OUT OF BONDAGE

Identifying and Breaking Control Spirits in the Church

Tim Mather

BCR Press

Copyright © 2005, 2017 by Tim Mather

www.timmather.com

All rights reserved, including the right to reproduce this book, or parts thereof, in any form except for the inclusion of brief quotations in a review. For more information, contact Bear Creek Ranch at www.bcrcamp.com.

Published by BCR Press an imprint of TrimVentures Publishing.
www.trimventures.com

ISBN 978-0-9987415-7-4

All Scriptures, unless otherwise indicated, are from the New International Version of the Bible.

Second Edition

for Katie
and all those whose lives
have been eternally altered by her life.

Table of Contents

Preface		*7*
1	It's All A Matter of Control	9
2	Control Spirits In the Church	14
3	Deliverance From Control Spirits	21
4	Disclaimers	27
5	Exposing the Control Spirit	35
6	Discovering the Control Spirit	42
7	Anger-Based Control Spirits	49
8	Fear-Based Control Spirits	56
9	Martyr-Based Control Spirits	63
10	Pleaser-Based Control Spirits	71
11	Sex-Based Control Spirits	79
12	The Spirit of Jezebel	89
13	Jezebel In Action	97
14	Ahab and Jezebel	104
15	The Luciferian Spirit	112
16	Weapons of Control Spirits	123
About the Author		*131*
Resources		*133*

Preface

Everybody has control issues. It is a natural part of life on this planet. But what if those normal human issues are being multiplied by destructive entities to demean people and destroy relationships? It is the most insidious bondage of all since we are unaware not only of its existence, but its devastating effects upon our lives.

The bondage created by the control spirit is the one of the worst sorts of evil. It permeates the fabric of our churches and our interpersonal relationships. Pastors are harassed by controlling people, husbands by control wives or vice versa, and our interpersonal relationships reveal no better witness than those left behind in the Kingdom of Darkness.

It's time someone put a stop to it.

Out of Bondage is not just a title, it's an aspiration. Who is truly living the "abundant life" of John 10:10? Why can't you? You have been kept in the dark long enough. The truth will indeed set you free, but there are some daunting paths between where you are and where you really want to go. You must face the true enemy without allowing fear to divert you from your goal. You must demand of yourself courage; you must set your sights higher than the Sunday morning sheepishness for which you have settled, lo these many years. Why not set your sights on excellence so that your Christian walk is a delight—you know like you make people at church believe you are living.

Most of us are in bondage and we don't even know it. We have created this little fantasy character for Sunday morning while living a mediocre existence the rest of the week. Isn't it time for Christianity to be fun like it's portrayed in the New Testament. Even when they were persecuted, *they rejoiced.* Maybe, just maybe it *can* be better than this.

Get out of bondage! And let the adventure begin!

Tim Mather

Chapter 1

It's All a Matter of Control

Somewhere Out In the Fog

"It's all a matter of control." He spoke the words quietly, as if off in the distance or somewhere out in a thick fog. I asked, "What does that mean, Lord?" There was only silence. This routine was repeated regularly over more than five years. Each time the words seemed closer and more distinct; each time I asked Him what it meant and each time there was silence.

"It's all a matter of control."

Not knowing the question made it impossible to discern what the answer meant. As the message became more distinct, I soon began to expect the Holy Spirit to speak it to my heart every time I went to prayer. After nearly six years of waiting for an explanation, I found myself saying, "It's all a matter of control" in response to someone asking me why someone acted the way he or she did. But it was not until 1993 that Father began to open my eyes to the magnitude of what He was revealing.

She Split My Lip

One day, my wife and I were having one of *those* discussions, you know, much too loud and *way* too emotional. Suddenly, she leaped at me with both fists flailing. One blow split my lower lip. As she punched, she shouted, "I will never tell you anything again! All you ever do is use it against me!" Somehow, I kept my composure and didn't strike back or even move to protect myself. Seeing me just standing there, she came at me again, but I was ready to block her little fists. As suddenly as she had attacked, she backed off, and stood there with her arms folded staring angrily at me. I took a breath and became aware that the presence of God had filled the room. I pointed my finger at the bed and commanded, "Sit down!" Miraculously, she sat down and folded her hands in her lap like a little girl. She had never obeyed me so swiftly, so I knew something was happening that was beyond both of us.

I asked her, "What other secrets have you kept from me?" Suddenly, out poured her life, most of which I had never heard: a life filled with sexual abuse and destruction beginning at age three by a non-family member and continuing into her early teenage years. She had never shared this with anyone, not even with me, her husband of eighteen years. As it came gushing out, the compassion of Jesus flowed over me. We began what would be a five-year long process of healing.

The Undeliverance

By this point, my wife and I had been in deliverance ministry for about twelve years, mostly conducted within our pastoral ministry. We had ministered deliverance to hundreds of people, and had seen them come to some levels of liberty. I had undergone deliverance myself in 1981, and she had been prayed over by a number of people throughout her walk with the Lord. Nearly every time a well-meaning pastor or Christian leader had ministered to her, he or she tried to set her free from a spirit of anger. After all, she was a very angry woman. However, she could never find the level of true freedom for which she so desperately sought. Her Christian life had become a system of strict rules and regulations intended to keep her free from sin, but it also kept her nearly devoid of joy. I called her my little Puritan because she was so perfectly religious and so obviously righteous. To the naked eye, she appeared to be the flawless Christian, which brings us back to the day she split my lip.

I Am Control

After she had finished opening her vaulted heart – so full of pain and rejection – we both came to the next logical step: she needed deliverance. We were scheduled to leave for a conference the following day, so during that time we shared the whole ordeal with my parents who were veteran pastors. The four of us left for the conference and agreed my father and mother should conduct the deliverance session. The Holy Spirit had already visited me and given me the names of the unclean spirits harassing my wife. However, I was instructed not to tell my father who they were. I was to only confirm what he would discern.

As my father conducted the session, he was reticent to say the name of the first demon he encountered. Afterward, he told us he was afraid she might leap up and split his lip for saying its name: a spirit of whoredom. He said it was not attached to her. It had been detached at the moment of her salvation. It was assigned to wait for the moment she gave in to sexual sin or walked away from God so he could reattach himself to her.

Over the next hour, he spoke the names of the demons I had written on my list and they were cast out. In the end, there was only one remaining: the ruling spirit over her life. He struggled for what seemed like an eternity to discern the spirit's name, but it remained hidden. It seemed the Holy Spirit had stopped speaking. He could still see it with his spiritual eyes, so he commanded it to look at him. In that moment, my wife began to gag, not just the dry heaves, but gagging as if something was choking the life out of her. My father commanded it to stop; it did not. He commanded the demon to leave; it would not. I was in a panic; I was about to be given the woman I thought I'd married and now she was going to be taken away from me?

Not on your life.

I quickly scratched on a piece of paper, "Command it to say its name!" My father read the note and vigorously shook his head. He was not going to do it. So, I scrambled from my perch and usurped his authority, commanding, "What is your name?" Out of her mouth came a voice so deep and raspy I knew she could not be pretending. It said, "I AM CONTROL!"

After we picked our jaws up from the floor, my dad commanded the unclean spirit of control to leave and it fled. We dealt with her wounds and loosed the anointing of the Holy Spirit upon her and waited to see the results.

RECOVERY FROM SPIRITUAL SURGERY

The next day, as we sat through a seminar on worship, the Holy Spirit began speaking to my heart. He clearly said that we must change my wife's name. When I asked why, the answer came very graciously and carefully. He said, "You will change her name to "Katie." Every time you hear this name spoken, it will serve as a rock of remembrance of what great things the Lord your God has done for you this day."

As I finished writing, I laid the book down on the table and began listening to the speaker. Just as we gave him our attention, he spoke the same words (he was sharing about the Israelites building an altar of remembrance at the crossing of the Jordan River into the Promised Land) I had just written in my notebook. My wife leaned over to me and whispered, "Do you think we should go back to the motel and make a big pile of stones in the room as a remembrance of what has happened?" I just shook my head and handed my book to her and she read what I had written. Then she closed the book, crying silently. From that moment, my wife's name has been "Katie." I always say, "She is my second wife, though she just happens to occupy the same body as my first wife."

Since that time there has been one revelation after another about what the Lord spoke to me so many years before: "It's all a matter of control."

Chapter 2

CONTROL SPIRITS IN THE CHURCH

A CHANGE IN FOCUS

The first revelations that came to us were concerning our own personal lives and how the spirit of control had twisted us into joyless, religious people. Soon, however, something else began to occur: others suffering from the same malady began appearing on our doorstep asking for help. This was initiated during a Sunday morning service in which we shared her testimony for the first time. We called it "Freedom From the Bondage of Shame." I went into graphic details about Katie's life and deliverance. To dramatize the sermon, I had handcuffed Katie before the service and asked her to participate in the worship team and do the announcements while bound in handcuffs. We wanted to demonstrate that she was able to worship, serve and minister – limited and hindered as she was – while denying the existence of her bondage. As we came to the end of the sermon, she knelt before the Lord with her bound hands lifted toward heaven. I took the handcuff key and set her free from her bondage while the worship team sang an old Bill Gaither song which begins, "Shackled by a heavy burden..."[1]

The next few minutes changed our lives forever. I turned to the congregation and extended a very specific, targeted invitation. I invited only those directly affected by sexual abuse in their own lives to respond. There were about a hundred adults in the room (the children were enjoying Kids' Church) and about seventy-five of them – both men and women – came forward. I later heard clearly on the sermon audiotape what I would say next. I had whispered, "Oh Lord, what do we do now?"

It took us more than six months just to meet with those who came forward. What we found completely changed the focus of our ministry. The church was full of damaged people, in this case, those who had been sexually abused before the age of eighteen. That may not be a revelation to you, but we believed people when they told us they were "fine" and "praise the Lord," they were "walking in freedom." In the years since that service, we have found nearly eighty percent of the adult female population in the church are victims of childhood sexual abuse, verbal abuse, physical abuse, emotional abuse, or any combination of these. The numbers for men are no better.

DEMONIZATION AND SEXUAL ABUSE

Having made the connection between sexual abuse and the presence of control spirits, we began intensive research to find the solution to their captivity. Sexual abuse, among a myriad of other traumatic events, is, nearly without exception, a doorway through which the demonic flows. We know that where spiritual darkness is found, demons have the legal right to inhabit that place (Jude 6). Demons require a doorway, that is, a legal right, to attach themselves to people. This can occur through a number of ways. First, it may happen through a generational curse line (Exodus 20:5). The sins of the father (and the mother) are passed down through the generational line just as surely as heart disease, distinctive facial features, or those weird toes that are "just like your father's." Children born under the curse of sin are subjected to the devastating effects of the sins of their ancestors. These effects produce enough spiritual darkness that demons have legal right to automatically inhabit that darkness.

Next, it may be through some others-imposed trauma such as sexual abuse, verbal abuse, neglect or the like. Finally, the doorway may be the sinful action of the person himself. By choosing to sin against themselves and Father, they provide spiritual darkness for the demons to inhabit.

THE SINNER'S PRAYER

When the person becomes born again, the weight of sin is wiped away, but often the effects of generational sins continue on. This happens because there is little or no recognition of the need for deliverance as part of the Good News of Jesus as stated in His mission statement found in Luke 4:18-19 KJV: *"The Spirit of the Lord is upon me, because he hath anointed me to preach the gospel to the poor; he hath sent me to heal the brokenhearted, to preach deliverance to the captives, and recovering of sight to the blind, to set at liberty them that are bruised, to preach the acceptable year of the Lord."*

These six parts of the Good News may not be assumed just because someone says "the sinner's prayer." In fact, the first part, *"preach the gospel to the poor,"* only ensures that the person's spirit is born again. The rest of the person, the soul (mind, will, and emotions) and the physical body remain under the effects of the curse spoken over Adam and Eve. When one becomes born again, one does not get a new body--even though many of us would be very grateful if that were the case. Neither does one receive a new mind, set of emotions, or will. Once born again, our mind, emotions, and will require continual renewing (Romans 12:1-2) as is shown in my book *Prophetic Deliverance*.

Demonization occurs in these last two portions of our being: body and soul. Therefore, the full effect of the Good News can only be had if the seeker receives the entire message. The message is only complete when the person's spirit is born again, and his/her broken emotions are healed, because one cannot grow up under the curse of sin and not be damaged in this area. Freedom must come to the person from the demonic influences that hinder growth. Demons subtly influence naïve Christians to remain in their damage and thereby influence them to unwittingly worship the Prince of the power of the air. Recovery of the spiritual sight relationship with Father must be made through the healing for our spiritual blindness. Then, our wounded and crushed spirits must find healing. Finally, the recoveree must know that pure acceptance and favor extended to them by Father.

The Western Church, assuming itself to be more "civilized" and "modern" than the Church in rest of the world, has entirely eliminated deliverance from its liturgy, practice, and ministry. Of course, the entire idea of demons having any sort of ability to affect mankind is foreign to most in our Western mindset. M. Scott Peck says:

> The concept of evil has been central to religious thought for millennia. Yet it is virtually absent from our science of psychology—which one might think would be vitally concerned with the matter. The major reason for this strange state of affairs is that the scientific and religious models have hitherto been considered totally immiscible—like oil and water, mutually incompatible and rejecting.[2]

Therefore, we can conclude that (if the Good News is comprised of the six parts as stated in the verse above) many who say, *"Lord, Lord!"* have missed the joy of knowing the freedom and liberty found in Jesus' promise: *"I have come that they may have life, and have it to the full"* (John 10:10). The percentage of Christians who are truly living their lives *"to the full"* is so small it could be argued that Christianity doesn't work in the real world and has become just another worthless philosophy.

Ask yourself this question: "Would the people who are closest to me describe me as living my life to the fullest?" Here is another one: "How many Christians do you know who are living the full life?" I grew up in the Church and I can count on the fingers of both my hands the number of Christians I have met who meet the criteria of John 10:10b.

The next question is obvious: "Why?" Why is there so little joy? Why so little victorious living among us? And, of course, how can so-called Christian people cheat their neighbor, commit adultery, perform business without integrity, be so angry, confused, suspicious, frightened, jealous, and mean?

I am convinced that the reason for the continuation of these problems is that we have not been given the privilege of knowing Jesus in the healing of our brokenness. Preachers throw sermons at us and expect us to be perfect, while we remain captive to the very things that enslaved us before we came to Christ. Preachers rant angrily about the evils of sin without really giving us the remedy, without revealing the privilege of the spiritual sight relationship, refusing to allow the laity to operate in the supernatural realm of prophetic dreams, visions and hearing the voice of the Good Shepherd. Little is being offered about knowing Jesus as the healer of our deep, secret wounds. We are encouraged to think positively, employ self-discipline, and all will be well. After it all, we feel we are the exceptions to the rule. Jesus' promises are for everyone but me.

The Church is in desperate need of real solutions. She has made converts instead of disciples. Jesus' command was to *"go and make disciples of all nations, baptizing them in the name of the Father and of the Son and of the Holy Spirit, and teaching them to obey everything I have commanded you. And surely I am with you always, to the very end of the age"* (Matthew 28:19-20). Today, we get them "saved" and consider the remainder of the Good News as automatic. It is not automatic. Disciples are learners who sit at the feet of Jesus to know Him in all He is.

What ails the Church cannot be cured by another sermon. Our disease can only be cured by finding the entirety of the Good News and putting it all into action. "I also believe that many

Christians with damaged emotions and unhealed memories need a special kind of inner healing to enable them to live victorious lives."[3]

THE ESSENTIALS OF CHRISTIANITY

As I presented in *Prophetic Deliverance*, deliverance ministry is not just another program of the Church like the worship team, Sunday School, or the youth group. "It is important to recognize that deliverance is the centerpiece of the entire message of salvation."[4] It is therefore an essential element of the salvation process as opposed to an optional ministry or one to be ignored altogether. So many times deliverance ministry is used only for those who are found flopping around on the floor or whose lives are so completely decimated that the devil must be involved. The truth, however, is not quite so dramatic. The demons who rule the Church have become as sophisticated and civilized as the people they harass. They have learned to refrain from overplaying their hand and revealing their presence. Instead, they work subtly, moving in the shadows. And, "since demons have not gone out of business, we should join our Lord and Savior in the business of proclaiming the gospel and setting men and free from Satan's bondage."5

Pastors throughout the Church are defeated and God's people are powerless. How is it that the very Body of Jesus Christ is so impotent and weak? How is it that less than two percent of the Church population ever leads another person to Christ? How is it that governing boards stand in opposition to the pastor's vision? Why does the organist hinder worship when it is not done exactly as she demands? Why is it that the people hate change--the very basis of the Christian experience--and hold to outdated and useless traditions of men?

The answer is simple: the full measure of the Good News has been withheld. Getting our spirit born anew is wonderful-- securing us a place for eternity--and the only place to begin, but the rest of the Good News is essential for living life to the full here.

Brokenhearted people lash out at others out of their skewed emotions. Captive people struggle endlessly against those things still ruling them. Blind Christians are relegated to paying the clergy to do all the work because they cannot see their own spiritual destiny. And wounded, crushed people endure religion with its rules and regulations because relationship is nonexistent. The destruction is so deep they are unable to enter into the rest.

Deliverance is not some weird ministry that should be kept out of the hands of the saints. Rather, it is one of the essentials of salvation itself. It is a right and a privilege of everyone who comes to Christ. Every sinner whose spirit gets born anew is entitled to healing for damaged emotions, spiritual blindness, and deep-seated wounds. Moreover, all believers are entitled to the miracle of deliverance as well.

LIGHT AT THE END OF YOUR TUNNEL

Those who have not undergone deliverance and healing as part of their salvation experience are subject to the influence and harassment of any number of demons. Katie was just such a person. She was not only a committed Christian, but she was a pastor's wife, a teacher in the church, and was even involved in deliverance ministry. However, the darkness hidden deep within her was fertile ground for demonic attachment. She had confessed her sins repeatedly, desperately attempting to find freedom, only to come to the conclusion that there must be something wrong with her that could not be touched by Father. After years of frustration, repentance, weeping and contrition, she finally accepted what had become the truth for her: this is as good as it gets.

Maybe this is what you have felt about yourself. We encourage you to read on. It may seem harsh at times, but there is healing in these pages.

Chapter 3

DELIVERANCE FROM CONTROL SPIRITS

FINDING DELIVERANCE IN THE ATONEMENT

Deliverance must be understood within the context of the atonement of Jesus. Jesus' mission statement is the complete working of the Cross. Receiving Jesus as our Savior is the first and most important step in the process, but it is a process rather than an event. The process of salvation must include all six portions of the mission statement, as laid out in Luke 4:18-19 KJV:

1. Cleansing sin and resulting acceptance into the family of God
2. Healing the brokenness in our emotions
3. Deliverance from the ruling darkness in our lives
4. The opening of our spiritual eyes to the realm of the spirit
5. Finding the joy of healing our crushed and wounded spirit
6. Discovering the Father has accepted each of us as His favorite

Many saints who are surely part of the family of God have been denied the full presentation of the Good News and remain broken, demonized, blind and crushed. This explains the ridiculous behavior found in every church: dissension, backbiting, fights, gossip, and a myriad of other things that are utterly contrary to the message of the Apostle John, *"If anyone says, 'I love God,' yet hates his brother, he is a liar. For anyone who does not love his brother, whom he has seen, cannot love God, whom he has not seen"* (I John 4:20).

Deliverance cannot be seen outside this context. Every believer must undergo deliverance as surely as he must be born again. Without it, parts of his heart remain unbelieving and, rather than living out *"I have come that they may have life, and have it to the full"* (John 10:10b)--he lives out *"we are of all men most miserable"* (I Corinthians 15:19b).

RECOVERING FROM BEING A HEATHEN

When one comes to Jesus, there will be a transformation. Our first clue is: *"Therefore, if anyone is in Christ, he is a new creation; the old has gone, the new has come!"* (II Corinthians 5:17). The problem is that the vast majority of Christians simply add God to their lives rather than finding themselves to be a new, alien creation.

The Western Church is guilty of watering down the message to make it palatable to the self-absorbed minds of the culture. By and large, it fails miserably to convey the truth that we are actually privileged to be completely altered by the experience of salvation and the subsequent Christian walk. When we are subjected to the full message of Luke 4:18-19, we are birthed into an entirely new race of people, no longer remaining who we were pre-Christ. We are a new creation. This creation did not exist in the Garden of Eden. It did not exist when Jesus walked the earth. At the day of Pentecost a new species appeared upon the earth.

Believers in Jesus are that new species.

Another clue to this new species is found in Romans 12:1-2 *"Therefore, I urge you, brothers, in view of God's mercy, to offer your bodies as living sacrifices, holy and pleasing to God--this is your spiritual act of worship. Do not conform any longer to the pattern of this world, but be transformed by the renewing of your mind. Then you will be able to test and approve what God's will is--his good, pleasing and perfect will."* When we get born again, the transformation of spirit is immediate and secures our place in the family of God. The rest of our being is then under attack by the presence of the divine in the core of our soulish areas.

That attack is designed to be progressive and prejudicial. The Holy Spirit of the Living God has been invited to take up residence and the rulership of who we are. His game plan is simple but comprehensive. Step one is dizzying: *"He must increase, but I must decrease"* (John 3:30 KJV). There is no room for self-absorbed living as he increases and we decrease in desires attitudes and function. We were designed for one active ruler and if it is Christ, self must be put away (Colossians 3:9 KJV).

So much is made of "who we are in Christ" when the real issue is clear: "Who is Christ in me?" Paul, under the instruction of the Holy Spirit wrote the antidote: *"I die every day--I mean that, brothers--just as surely as I glory over you in Christ Jesus our Lord"* (I Corinthians 15:31). Successful Christianity is defined by these words: *"I die every day."* This death is assured by our willing sacrifice to the divine fire of the Holy Spirit as we first offer our physical bodies to His destruction through worship. Worship is a key to recovering from being a heathen. As we occupy our soulish area-our mind, our emotions and our will-with who HE is, we find a decrease of the self-centered culture that has been bred into us and an expansion of who He is in us.

Reread Romans 12:1-2 above and see it as actual rather than some virtual theological or philosophical exercise. As the sacrifice of our bodies is made plain, our soulish areas come under attack. There must be a continual transformation in the realm of our mind, our emotions and our will. The presence of God in us is making an ambitious demand. It is an all-out invasion and we must participate in the destruction of who we are in favor of who He is. Only then are we able to find out what He wants and what His plans are for us.

CONTROL SPIRITS AND HIS GOOD, PLEASING AND PERFECT WILL

Due to the unique nature of their demonization, those influenced by control spirits seem to find it particularly difficult to submit to the dismantling of who they were before Christ. Everyone who comes into the Kingdom of God experiences some ruling issues swept away by the cleaning service known as the Blood of the Lamb. We are cleansed from our sin by His blood, but the effects of sin frequently remains behind. Lee was driving home after a night of drugs and drinking. He was under the impression that he could make it home down the road he had traveled a thousand times. However, he lost control of the car and crashed headlong into a tree. The car was so utterly destroyed witnesses could not even tell what kind of car it was. His door came open and he fell out of the car and down into a creek where he laid semiconscious for the rest of the night. When he was found, he had nearly bled out, and had multiple broken bones. In the years following, Lee came to Christ and was born again. However, the scars remain, the pain in his joints remain, and many other physical effects remain. His sins were forgiven, but the physical effects of his sin remained.

The soulish consequences of sin frequently remain, as well. We have all heard the testimony of the person who says, "I was an alcoholic before I met Jesus but when I got saved I never wanted to touch another drop." The Blood of the Lamb swept the urge away. How is it possible then that some other person may share, "I have been born again for several years but somehow I still battle the desire to drink." The fact that Father *"does not show favoritism"* (Acts 10:34) precludes the second person from actually being less loved by Father, though he certainly may feel that it is true. This points us to the only conclusion: the effects of sin continue after salvation when the entire force of Luke 4:18 is not applied.

For years the Church has watered down the message of the Good News so it could be sold to the self-centered culture of the Western world. In the process, we have received thousands upon thousands of newborn believers into the Kingdom without applying the rest of the Message to their plight. They remain under the rulership of the trauma, the damage of their prior existence, wondering why Father and the Church let them down. That damage provides enough darkness for demonization to remain even after their spirit has been born again.

THE EFFECTS OF THE PARTIAL GOOD NEWS

Without the *"he hath sent me to heal the brokenhearted,"* the *"to preach deliverance to the captives,"* and the *"to set at liberty them that are bruised"* portions of the Good News activated in their lives, the victim of a control spirit is still subject to its influence. Their emotions remain out of control unless who they were is completely destroyed by the Holy Spirit and rebuilt in a healthy, submitted balance. They remain captive to the control spirit's influence because, when they received Jesus, no one took them through deliverance and uncovered the presence of this ruling spirit over them. Their deep brokenness was overlooked in favor of a partial presentation of the Good News alleging an automatic sweeping away of the damage. As the first portion of Luke 4:18 must be pursued for salvation to occur, so must each portion of the rest of the Good News be pursued, to facilitate wholeness.

DATA ORIENTED CHRISTIANITY

The fact of the matter is that our doctrinal teaching has

become so data-oriented that the healing aspect of the Good News is almost always forgotten. We are taught to memorize facts and figures about the Bible and the doctrines of the institutional Church without developing the necessary relationship required in the family of God. As Robert Lund says in his book, *The Way Church Ought To Be*, "Right out of the gate, the Christian Church was born in community."[6] Within that community is the only atmosphere where wholeness can germinate and prosper.

Some people survive and even appear to flourish without the rest of the Good News, however, the majority of the Body of Christ is walking in brokenness and devastation. This fact unveils the real purpose of writing on this sensitive and culturally taboo subject. Unless we care for the people caught in the web of theological deception that insists they should ignore the damage that still rules them, the Church will continue its spiral into the irrelevant obscurity in which we find ourselves.

Chapter 4

Disclaimers

A Note of Caution

Before moving to the next section, it seems prudent to address several disclaimers intended to calm what might be a violent reaction to what is being said.

First, it must be understood that those infected by (this we will call "hosting") control spirits are rarely aware these unclean spirits are resident, although, the people around them are usually acutely aware. This phenomenon is due to the nature of control spirits. The reason my wife's deliverance required the demon's voice to be heard by her was so she would believe it was real. She testifies today that she would never have believed it without that empirical evidence. She had worked in deliverance ministry for twelve years by this point and had seen many set free. We violated our own rules regarding the restriction of manifestations during deliverance in order that she would recognize something had been ruling her. Of course, for most, such evidence is unnecessary.

We knew she carried an excessive amount of anger, but we assumed "that's just the way she is." This same simple principle proves itself time and again: those hosting control spirits are so busy bringing their lives into some semblance of order they are unable to see it for themselves. The use of control as a survival mechanism is a destructive doorway, giving unclean spirits a toehold and allowing them to wreak havoc on an already broken person until the toehold is a stronghold. Ultimately, controlling behavior destroys relationships, especially when it is multiplied by demonic influences.

LIFE TO THE FULL

The second area we must address concerns our handling of those carrying control spirits. It must be clear that these people are victims. We are not berating or belittling people for sport. We are not bringing accusations or slandering hardworking, committed Christian men and women just because my wife went through something weird. On the contrary! We love these people dearly and are committed to seeing them out of bondage and functioning in freedom. This book is not just the testimony of one woman's escape from bondage. Instead, it serves as a testimony of nearly a thousand women who have found the reality of *"life to the full"* (John 10:10). It is also the testimony of several hundred men who have found the same thing. Please do not hear us calling you names or questioning your relationship with Jesus. Instead, hear the voice of the Father, in our words, urging, "Be free."

STRONG WOMEN

Another area of concern is the possible accusation that we may be attacking women simply because they are strong, outspoken or intelligent. Nothing could be further from the truth. Katie and I have raised three daughters who are powerful in anointing, have strong opinions, and are tremendous assets to their husbands and to the Lord. We are not trying to create a subspecies of "June Cleavers" walking around in perfect attire waiting for their "Ward" to come home from work to a spotless house. All of our daughters have gone to college, now work, participate in ministry, and think for themselves. We have seen each of them go through deliverance with our teams and rid themselves of generational curse lines due to the control spirit from their mother. But, contrary to fears expressed by some wounded women, they have not degraded into "Stepford wives."

Many strong, intelligent, gifted women are a vital part of our ministry--beginning with my wife--and they serve Father with gladness. The truth is this: those who were manipulated by control spirits and then are set free tend to become some of the best workers, preachers, teachers, intercessors, and friends for whom we could ever ask.

RECOVERY TIME

The next point relate to the length of the recovery time. Deliverance can be equated to major surgery. Though some make it just another spiritual event, we have found the recovery time after deliverance is as crucial as deliverance itself. First let us define what we mean by "recovery time." Using the metaphor above, it is the time following surgery when the medical staff cares for the patient and facilitates the healing process. This begins as a careful, loving time, but, if you have ever experienced recovery from surgery, it quickly changes into a veritable demand for healing. The first demand is that the patient must sit up--a simple thing for a well person, a horrifying prospect for one who has just been cut open. Then, it's "Get out of bed." This assault is followed by a demand to start walking, or rather, a strange sort of shuffling down the hospital hallway. The members of the nursing staff, who were so gentle at first, now appear to hound the patient into creating more pain by demanding movement.

However, the worst is yet to come: physical therapy. This part of the surgery experience is often arduous, painful, stressful, and is frequently torturous. A physical therapist may appear to be an expert in medieval torture as he massages the sore, atrophied muscles and forces them to move after the period of inactivity. The physical therapy room of a hospital, though a place of real healing and recovery, emits a variety of cries, moans and angry retorts.

This typifies the Wholeness Process. We encourage the deliverance recoveree to deal with their warped paradigms by bringing them face to face with Father's truth. They need to reach into those hurt places that have never seen the light of day and allow in the light of Jesus. It is the process of recovery not so much from deliverance, but recovery from being a heathen. It is the definition of what it means to be a disciple. The pain comes from finding that much of what you believe about the world, and more importantly about yourself, is warped, skewed or completely false.

It can be a painful process.

In the typical institutional Church setting, when people are converted to Christ there is no demand for any such commitment. Intellectual assent can be had without the surgeon's scalpel cutting and scraping every portion of one's being. Luke 4:18 Christianity moves beyond mentally agreeing Jesus is Who He says He is, into a total dismantling of who we are through deliverance and healing. Some believe this can be done on an outpatient basis, a simple procedure, allowing the disciple to be who he or she has always been. The wonderful and terrible news is: *"For those God foreknew he also predestined to be conformed to the likeness of his Son"* (Romans 8:29). There is violence in these words.

THE LIFE AND TIMES OF A COOKIE

"To be conformed to the likeness" can be likened to the creation of a cookie. Imagine you are the dough. There you are, fat and happy in your doughy existence, when, smack, someone hits you with all his might, pressing and stretching you into some alien form. You consider the pain and the fact you "didn't

grow up that way" and give thanks that, at least you are still a big lump of dough. But then it hits you, literally! You are rudely introduced to the rolling pin. The pain is excruciating, stretching you into a shape completely outside your comfort zone. Soon, you retain little resemblance to that carefree blob of dough you once were. Your only comfort is in the reality that you are still in one piece and you are still dough.

It must be enough. Oh, please, God, let it be enough! And then it appears . . . the cookie cutter. This cannot be an expression of love. After all, God is love; God is a passive hippy who sits around heaven contemplating all things peaceful and loving. Therefore, the cookie cutter must be from the devil himself! It is most certainly going to destroy everything you have worked to become.

As you watch, down comes the cutter held in the hand of Someone so much greater than yourself that you have no concept of Him or His world. The pain is beyond description. Parts of you that have been dear to your personality, character, and your very essence are being cut away. Only the part that fits within the cutter is left. The rest is being set aside, discarded. As you peer helplessly at yourself you realize you don't look like yourself anymore.

You look like something else.

Soon the memories of the pain begin to fade as you acclimate to this new thing. It seems that *"the old has gone"* and that something *"new has come"* (II Corinthians 5:17). You begin to become comfortable in this new creation. This must be the goal for which you have endured. Still there seems to be something else happening. Your heart races.

"What exactly is an oven, anyway? And why should it have any effect upon me?" The horrifying truth dawns on you: the something else is headed for the burning depths of the oven. "Oh Lord, please deliver me. The devil is attacking me." That's it: this must be spiritual warfare! "Stand with me in this, brother."

Still the gaping jaws of the oven move closer and closer until you are swallowed up. Feeling confident that you can endure the darkness into which you have been plunged, a bead of sweat appears on your little cookie brow as you look down to find that this oven thing is full of fire. "This cannot be of God!" And you spend the next few years of your life fighting the effects of the fire, rebuking, naming and claiming, or praying fervently, convinced success cannot be found in the bowels of the fiery furnace. "After all," you profess confidently, "when I got saved I understood that my problems were over and everything is supposed to be peace and love."

Thankfully, this fire is only for a season and, mercifully, the season finally comes to an end. The cool air moving across the kitchen table comes as a refreshing wind. Now out of the darkness and heat of the oven, you take a moment to consider who you have become. You don't resemble anything you ever dreamed of or desired to be. Though, on the inside, you are still soft and pliable, you now realize you are no longer doughy, but something quite different. Instead of your wonderfully pale, gooey exterior, you are a reconditioned tough, crispy entity entirely dissimilar from anything familiar in your pre-oven world.

Quite satisfied you have achieved the highest spiritual honor ever (after all, you are now, more than ever, conformed to the image of His Son), you discover what you have endured is only the preparation, the basic training for your true destiny. The destiny of every believer is an intimacy with Father beyond singing a few songs and hearing a few sermons. What does it mean in your cookie world? It means a gapping abyss framed by lips, teeth, tongue and throat. This is the definition of the Apostle Paul's words: *"I die every day"* (I Corinthians 15:31). It is not mere religious assent that, sure, God is God and I'm not. It is most certainly being devoured by the One Who made you, molded you, sanctified you (the cookie cutter), put you through the fire, and refreshed you. This all leads up to true Christianity:

intimacy. Father is about the task of restoring the intimate relationship He enjoyed with Adam and Eve to you.

Remaining who we are opposes who we can become in Christ. When we know what "in Christ" means, we gladly submit to Him devouring us.

Endless Discomfort

The greatest deterrent to finding wholeness is the length of time it takes to heal. Apparently, Christians are the single most impatient group on the planet. We are like the little child who wants his stuff and wants it NOW! The active time of recovery after a normal deliverance session may be several years. It may take victims of control spirits much more time, maybe even double the norm to find complete healing. The reason for such a distinction is this: control spirits have such a high level of influence on their victim that the deliverance and wholeness process may alter the personality of the victim. This has been confirmed to us by a psychiatrist who warned a mutual client to stay away from us, "Because if they really do what they say, it will change your personality." Of course, this is impossible in the natural world since one's personality is set and firm at around four or five years of age. Then, we are stuck with that personality for our lifetime. Isn't it interesting that deliverance releases the hand of Father to do the impossible?

So, if you consider moving in the direction of deliverance, understand that recovery may take some time, in fact, it may be a tough few years. On the other hand, the easy Gospel that has been preached in the West has produced weak, failing, impotent Christians because we have been led to believe we only need to add God to our lives. Somehow I don't think Jesus was kidding when He said, *"If anyone would come after me, he must deny himself and take up his cross and follow me"* (Matthew 16:24).

When we come to Christ, we cannot simply add God to the balance of our existing life. On the contrary, in coming to Christ, we therefore give up all rights to hold on to who we are. Is salvation a free gift? We hear it preached as such so often. Well, if this is a free gift, it is the one that will cost you everything you are, think, and own. *"For whoever wants to save his life will lose it, but whoever loses his life for me will find it"* (Matthew 16:25) is the picture of being completely devoured by Him. Jesus paid the entire cost for our salvation; it is true! But in receiving that free gift we are privileged to *"be conformed to the likeness of his Son,"* (Romans 8:29) and that costs us everything.

Under the umbrella of these disclaimers, we will begin to uncover the nature and character of the spirit of control haunting the pews of our churches and the hallways of our homes.

Chapter 5

Exposing the Control Spirit

Covert Demonization

Those hosting control spirits are seldom aware an unclean spirit is present. This is due to the nature of the control spirit. The spirit may connect with the victim through one of a variety of ways. First, the person may be demonized through a generational curse line. Just as alcoholism, abuse, mental illness, or physical illness can be passed generation to generation, so too, are control spirits. In many cases, family lines reveal that each generation may manifest a control spirit, though they may be a different type.

Next, a person may be opened to demonic infestation as a result of trauma imposed by other people. The list of possible trauma includes any sort of abuse, including physical, sexual, mental, or verbal, being terrified, some sort of crippling accident, disease, or any other pungent event. Such an incident opens the doorway for demons to attach to the darkness created in the soulish arena as control behaviors develop.

Finally, people may be demonized by their own sinful actions. The presence of any spiritual darkness furnishes ample legal right for an unclean spirit to take up residence. Each person is responsible for his own actions before Father.

Committing sins against Him once again immerses the spirit in spiritual darkness. As the darkness grows, the risk of demonic influence and infestation grows concurrently. Demons have been authorized habitation of any spiritual darkness according to Jude 6 – *"And the angels who did not keep their positions of authority but abandoned their own home—these he has kept in darkness, bound with everlasting chains for judgment on the great Day."*

Since each human has been born within the parameters of the kingdom of darkness, the presence of such darkness is natural, comfortable, and familiar. The demonic realm is aware of this fact and they exploit it. The result is the covert presence of demons influencing, controlling, and manipulating people who are mostly or completely unaware of their presence. Therefore, the Holy Spirit of the Living God is tasked with unmasking the demonic and directing the willing toward deliverance.

DISTINGUISHING THE CONTROL SPIRIT FROM OTHER DEMONIZATION

Our deliverance method is different from others in that we interview neither the client nor the demon to diagnose the presence of a particular unclean spirit. The reasons are simple. First, if the deliverance team interviews the person as to their opinion, the tendency of the team will be to take that natural knowledge and make use of it in the session. The dilemma here is we humans are seldom able to see ourselves objectively and frequently make judgments based upon symptoms rather than upon the source of the problem. Additionally, the deliverance team, being human, will limit themselves to the information given by the client and come to their conclusion based upon the natural understanding. Prophetic Deliverance does not allow room for these two problems. Instead, the team is required to rely solely upon the Holy Spirit's diagnosis without the introduction of any information provided by the client.

Second, should the team rely upon what the demons say in

response to questions, the deliverance process will be impossible to complete. Any deliverance method that interviews a demon is flawed. It is flawed because demons are liars, just like their father Satan. *"You belong to your father, the devil, and you want to carry out your father's desire. He was a murderer from the beginning, not holding to the truth, for there is no truth in him. When he lies, he speaks his native language, for he is a liar and the father of lies"* (John 8:44). How can a deliverance team circumvent the native tongue of lies? Certainly, under great duress a demon may speak truth, but to rely upon this rare occurrence makes for a clumsy, inaccurate, ineffective deliverance.

Beyond the deception lies a hidden danger. In conversing with demons, one must be acutely aware that their motivation is to seduce us away from the truth. This is accomplished through appealing to our intellect and pride. I have seen many participate in deliverance ministry who take great pride in what they have seen and heard. *"Do not let anyone who delights in false humility and the worship of angels disqualify you for the prize. Such a person goes into great detail about what he has seen, and his unspiritual mind puffs him up with idle notions. He has lost connection with the Head, from whom the whole body, supported and held together by its ligaments and sinews, grows as God causes it to grow"* (Colossians 2:18-19).

Jesus' response to the excitement of His disciples returning from their mission trip is clearly opposed to this seduction: *"The seventy-two returned with joy and said, 'Lord, even the demons submit to us in your name.' He replied, 'I saw Satan fall like lightning from heaven. I have given you authority to trample on snakes and scorpions and to overcome all the power of the enemy; nothing will harm you. However, do not rejoice that the spirits submit to you, but rejoice that your names are written in heaven'"* (Luke 10:17-20). We urge our teams to focus upon the freedom found only in Jesus instead of dwelling upon war stories of the demonic.

The other way Prophetic Deliverance is different is that we do not use a list of demons to diagnose which one is present. We have encountered thousands of different demons operating under thousands of functional names. It would be impossible to provide a detailed list. After these many years of doing deliverance, we still encounter demons we have never encountered before. If we had confined ourselves to previously compiled list, we would have misidentified the demon and would have left the person without freedom. In view of this, we do not make lists. Instead, we simply listen to what the Holy Spirit has to say and we act accordingly.

THE EXCEPTION PROVING THE RULE

Though we are firmly opposed to making lists of demons, we take this opportunity to break our own rules and present a detailed understanding of a specific class of unclean spirits. The reason we make this exception is that demonization by control spirits is vastly different from any other type of infestation. The difference lies in how the demon operates. All victims of demonization have one thing in common: the demon affects them. It may affect them through infirmity, through mental duress or confusion; it may hinder their spiritual walk or multiply their fears. Whatever the operation, the demon always affects the person internally and the host is aware there is a problem. The affects of demonization are always directed toward the person hosting the demon. Others may see the issue and be aware there is a problem. However, the attack is inward and is focused entirely against the host.

Control spirits use the above operation as well, but add an additional operation. The primary focus of a control spirits attack is outward. This means the host may not even be aware of the control spirit's presence because it may never attack him. In fact, in walking out the recovery process with hundreds of such victims, we have found that, not only did the spirit seldom overtly attack them, its operation is received as a benefit to the host. While this opposes the normal operation of an unclean spirit, it is nevertheless the case.

In the case of the victim whose demonization is through the generational curse line, the labor of the control spirit is entirely interwoven into the psyche and personality of the person. Therefore, the victim will be unaware of the problem because it has been within them from conception. The control issue is then understood to be a personality issue as opposed to the spiritual issue it really is.

In the case of trauma-imposed demonization, the work of the demon will be to inhabit the fear of life-out-of-control and to assist in bringing the victim's life under control. The resulting opinion of the host will be that the demon's activity is a place of safety instead of a place of attack. The demon will provide comfort and safety in exchange for the right to attack, manipulate, and control those around the host. Therefore, the host of a control spirit will experience demonization in exactly the opposite manner of all other types of demonization.

While most other demonized persons know the effects of the demon as entirely negative, the host of a control spirit will be unconvinced of his own demonization because the inward focused operation of the demon appears to be positive in nature. The demon counterfeits safety, comfort, and independence to keep the person self-reliant and needing no one.

It is clear this goes beyond being a strong person. The demon creates the illusion that all is under control and anything challenging his host must be eliminated. This is why the victim may appear to be aloof, arrogant, dismissive, or combative. Should anything stand in his way, the host is trained by the demon for either fight or flight. Depending upon the particular type of control spirit, either of these options is acceptable, and the definitions of the words "fight" and "flight" change. These two words make up the repertory of coping mechanisms for the host, thereby, appearing to help the host rather than being defined as a demonic attack.

Recovery From the Influence of a Control Spirit

Generally, those recovering from demonic influence will find an initial honeymoon period where they may experience positive results. This is followed by the testing period in which the client will experience apparent relapses into learned behavior and patterns. But, with some effort in the pursuit of Father, they quickly flow through the test and move out into good growth in their spiritual life.

Again, it must be understood, that the recoveree from a control spirit is in a category all his/her own. The first reaction of many who find deliverance from control spirits is disbelief. Because the person is probably unaware of the demon or the behaviors it has brought into his/her life, many find it unbelievable that such a thing is true. We have had a variety of responses to the diagnosis and casting out control spirits, from violent anger to shame.

One such case involved a pastor's wife who the team unanimously diagnosed as a control spirit. Her initial reaction was to stare unbelievingly at me. From there she went home and cried all night. Sometime the next day she reappeared at the office, still weeping, very angry and mortified at what we had done. She sat down and did her best to understand what I was explaining to her about her condition. She calmed down and asked to see others of our team. After they confirmed what I had said, she went away even more angry.

Sometime the following week, she was still trying to talk her way out of what she'd experienced and mentioned it to the senior pastor of the church during their staff meeting. She asked him whether he thought she had been a controller and his response floored her. He said, "Yes, of course. I have known that for years."

She had never known what she was. However, everyone who had to work with her, her family and friends all knew she was extremely controlling. The spirit had not affected her, but it had affected everyone else.

Often, it is important for the recoveree of a control spirit, whether male or female, to enter individual counseling with a qualified counselor to assist them through this most difficult period. They will be extremely vulnerable and fearful in this new world that seems completely out of control. The necessity of relinquishing control behaviors will be a difficult but essential transition in order for healing to occur.

The length of recovery time depends upon the determination of the individual to heal and thereby purposefully eliminate the existence of control behaviors. The need to control is a fruitless effort to protect one's woundedness. In essence, it is saying, "Jesus, I cannot trust you to heal me, so I am going to protect myself." It is denying Christ's provision in Luke 4:18-19. The recoveree should pursue the truth of his/her condition and face the facts concerning the open doorways to demonization and submit his/her control behaviors, distorted beliefs and wounds to the healing work of Jesus Christ. He/she should also participate in anointed worship where Father's healing flows as His presence is experienced. A small group in which personal recovery can be shared, celebrated and encouraged is very important. We encourage him/her to stay in contact with those equipped to pray for spiritual, mental, and emotional wounds. Public church services may only serve to isolate recoverees during this time and, though he/she may attend, this should not be the sole source of his/her recovery support system.

Chapter 6

DISCOVERING THE CONTROL SPIRIT

EXCAVATION

After Katie's deliverance we began the slow and arduous process of separating what was demonic training and influence from who Katie really was. This unclean spirit had been resident since conception-this being a case of a generational curse line-so we had no pre-demonization model for which to strive. We had no books to point the way; we had no teaching to make the end visible from the beginning. We only knew that there was someone new on the horizon that we must pursue.

The process we initiated was what we would later label the Path to Wholeness. We didn't know what we were looking for, only that the Holy Spirit was leading us through. During the first six months, we rummaged through every minute detail of Katie's life and tried to find the Lord in there somewhere. Katie was obliged to examine her life from top to bottom, her responses, her reactions, her views, her beliefs and her values.

IDENTIFYING THE SPIRIT

Katie's sense that her life was out of control laid the groundwork in her personality for her to be a controller. The abuse had opened the doorway for a paradigm conducive to the demonic.

In an effort to avoid being hurt, some people constantly try to maintain control of others and dominate the situations they face. They have become skilled in exercising control by dispensing approval or disapproval, unwilling to let others be themselves and make their own decisions without their consent. Because such people are actually very insecure, lack of control is an unacceptable threat to them.[7]

We discovered Katie had been victimized not only by her abusers, but also by unclean spirits inhabiting the spiritual darkness created by the trauma associated with sexual abuse. We took several months to consider how these spirits had manipulated her, the people around her, our ministry, our children, and me. It became clear others were under the influence of the same type of spirit as she had been. The Lord began sending them to us for help.

Our first task was to identify the nature and character of the spirit who called itself "control." Demons are counterfeiters; they are trying to fulfill the declaration of their ruler when he said, *"I will make myself like the Most High"* (Isaiah 14:14). Therefore, they know the "name" is the key to spiritual authority whether in the Kingdom of God or the Kingdom of Darkness. *"That at the name of Jesus every knee should bow, in heaven and on earth and under the earth, and every tongue confess that Jesus Christ is Lord, to the glory of God the Father"* (Philippians 2:10-11).

Once we have the name of the unclean spirit, we, according to their own hierarchal law, have authority over them. This name is what we call a "functional name" as opposed to a proper name. The functional name reveals the particular type of activity they use to manipulate their victims. For example, a spirit of fear's name is not "Larry Fear." Rather, it is fear that this spirit is using to exercise control over and through the victim.

This particular spirit gave its name as "control." Our research quickly began to uncover the nature of this type of spirit. The victims who came to us for help appeared to exhibit very similar characteristics. As we watched, prayed deliverance for them, and cared for them, we found there were several distinct areas of control being exercised. Though we have refrained from using lists of demons for diagnosing their presence within the deliverance setting, we have discovered that control spirits reveal themselves within such well-defined, narrow parameters they could be categorized. As these categories were exposed, it became clear that at the end of the spectrum was found a category we began to identify as "Jezebelian spirits."

At this point, we had not read any books on the topic, nor had we attended conferences or heard any sermons about Jezebelian spirits. In fact, we were unaware anyone else was researching this subject. In the nearly nine years following our introduction to these spirits, we have cast out hundreds of control spirits, assisted in the healing of hundreds of people set free from their grasp, and noted what it takes to recover entirely from their influence. Though we use Katie's testimony as an example, her experience was only the beginning of the adventure.

THE BASIC TYPES OF CONTROL SPIRITS

What follows is the result of over a decade of hands-on research involving those victimized by control spirits. There appears to be six basic types of control spirits and it's important they be defined and distinguished in order that the recovery process may be specific and targeted. Here is the list:

1. Anger-based control spirits
2. Fear-based control spirits
3. Martyr-based control spirits
4. Pleaser-based control spirits
5. Sex-based control spirits
6. Jezebelian/Luciferian spirits

The first five may be identified as control spirits, while the last category is a compilation of all five. Any of these spirits may infest either a man or a woman. The last category is the only where a distinction is necessary. This will be more fully explained later.

People feel free to inaccurately call a strong woman, "Jezebel" when she might be hosting a control spirit or may simply possess a strong personality. This tactic is one of manipulation and must not be tolerated. Not all strong women are demonized and not all control spirits are spirits of Jezebel. To arbitrarily label someone as having a Jezebelian spirit is to unfairly characterize and demean her. A deliverance session is the only adequate context in which to diagnose whether a Jezebelian spirit is present. In any other situation, the host of the Jezebelian spirit will attack and destroy anyone who exposes her. Be careful not to allow yourself or others to paint someone with this label. It is never redemptive and is often lethal to the accuser outside the deliverance context.

DEFINING A CONTROL SPIRIT

The spirit requires a specific mode of operation to exercise control over the host and over those connected to the host. This necessitates identifying the particular base of operations out of which the spirit works. Therefore, the control spirits listed above are defined as anger-based or fear-based. These spirits simply employ anger or fear as the controlling weapon.

Out of this base of operations, the demon will manipulate

both the host and those with whom they come in contact. In a normal case of demonization, the demon's mode of operation is to focus inwardly. He harasses his host; attempts to control him/her and uses all the resources at his disposal to make life miserable for his host, to the end that his victim turns from his/her pursuit of Father and returns to his/her natural state of darkness. Everything the unclean spirit does attempts to break the strong tower inhabited by Father.

However, there are two primary expressions of the control spirit as opposed to normal demonization. First, the unclean spirit controls the host in the same manner as ordinary demonization. But the person afflicted by a control spirit will exhibit a second, more powerful aspect of their demonization. The unclean spirit will be able to control people around the host. This is an external manifestation of the spirit. Not only is the host demonized, the people who surround the person--spouse, family members, coworkers, friends-are demonized by the external portion of the spirit harassing the host. The closer the connection to the host, the more the spirit is able to control them without leaving their assignment to the host.

Should the host of an anger-based control spirit be married, the husband will most often be a quiet, soft-spoken man who knows how to take orders from his wife. The intense anger she manifests will take a severe toll on the marriage. Therefore, a large percentage of women hosting control spirits may be divorced one or more times.

THE ATTACKER HAS THE POWER

In the case of Katie and those like her—those whose demonization has been initiated by or exacerbated by any sort of abuse--the fundamental motivation of the control spirit is to protect the person from perceived attack. This derives from the initial infestation doorway that made the person feel out of control. Her sexual abuse first took place at age three and continued until she turned the tables and began sexually abusing boys during her teen years. At the moment of extreme vulnerability, the victim is faced with one agonizing fact, which, though seldom verbalized, becomes the drumbeat of his/her heart for the rest of his/her life. The attacker is usually bigger in size, older and more manipulative than the victim. Therefore, the victim is made to understand that, no matter how hard he/she resists, no matter how much he/she does not want it to happen, the attacker has the power. There it is in black and white: the attacker has the power.

From that moment, the victim's life is consumed with regaining control. Can it be that simple? Indeed. As this unfolds you will find there is nothing so consuming as the need to have life make sense in an orderly, controlled fashion. Whatever the event is that opens the door for the control spirit to come, whether it is some sort of abuse, a generational curse line, or his or her own action, keeping life in some semblance of control becomes the driving force.

Now life is absorbed by who has control.

CONTROL SPIRITS HATE AUTHORITY

In our model of the sexual abuse victim, the perpetrator is most often male. In the case of incest, especially by the father or older brother, the effect is multiplied. In any case, the attacker becomes the object of obsession for the victim. The obsession is focused upon the person in authority because he has the power to harm at will, and the only safe place for the victim of the control spirit is in a position of authority. Therefore, anything or anyone that stands in a place of authority is a threat and must be eliminated. The victim will seek to rise into authority for safety and security.

The response to a person in authority will vary according to the particular type of control spirit the victim hosts and what their coping mechanisms provide as the best weapons to fend them off or destroy them. In the context of these weapons, the host may refuse or be unable to reconcile with issues of abuse so denial of their victimization offers a facade of safety. What follows are four examples of weapons against the use of authority upon a person hosting a control spirit:

- **Anger** - The victim will get angry without provocation and decide, how ever subconsciously, they do not like the person in authority. They will escape from under the authority or attack and destroy the person in authority and become the authority themselves.
- **Humor** - The victim will constantly make light of the situation and/or the person so as to deter the exercise of authority and their uneasiness with it.
- **Gaining Promotion** - Those with control spirits only flourish when they are in authority. So, they will do what ever it takes so that they and no other is in control. In the church, they may appear to be more spiritual than others, more gifted, more anointed. They seek the highest levels of the church authority structure from which to wield their power, using that power to spiritually abuse.
- **Befriending** - They may be the ones who quickly come along side those in authority in order to gain authority of their own. Leaders should be aware of this tactic and be very careful to prove anyone who too quickly comes along side.
- **Codependency** – Hosts of control spirits often use the control within the pendulum opposites of the feigned helpless dependent, or the fixer, rescuer, and savior.

Certainly, there are many other ways these spirits work, but these few examples will help us to understand the elementary truth.

Chapter 7

ANGER-BASED CONTROL SPIRITS

ANGER-BASED CONTROL SPIRITS

An Anger-based control spirit multiplies the natural anger the person harbors, whether consciously or subconsciously, toward any out-of-control aspects of life. In the instance of a sexually abused woman, the lack of control she experienced while enduring the abuse is enough trauma to create a doorway for demonic influence. The control spirit attaches itself to the darkness created by the trauma and uses the natural response of the victim as the springboard into higher and higher levels of anger.

It is important to understand that demons are not creative beings. Therefore, they cannot create anything, either externally or internally. Instead, they inhabit the dark nature of the person and multiply what they find. In the instance of the sexual abuse victim, the spirit takes the relatively small level anger he feels toward his attacker and multiplies it into a whirlwind of anger that might come out against anything or anybody.

The victim of an Anger-based control spirit has a burning furnace within that may explode at any moment, for the minutest reason. Often, the person does not even have a concept of how much anger is amassed. However, when released, this anger will nearly always be disproportionate for the situation.

Humor As a Cover

Many victims of this type of spirit work very hard at covering up the overflow of anger with humor. Humor is extremely effective in masking the truth that they are very angry most of the time. However, there will always be a "tell" in the kind of humor employed. It will often be biting satire or sarcasm directed against others or even against themselves. Frequently, hosts of Anger-based control spirits are the life of the party, quick-witted and bright, someone who keeps everyone laughing. Of course, this is a camouflaging mechanism for the dark, even malevolent anger that rules them.

Fearlessness

Additionally, many of those hosting Anger-based control spirits seemingly know no fear. Their anger is so consuming that they effectively eliminate all the natural fear safeguards normal people possess. Often, they may not be afraid of anything. They dare to do anything and seldom experience natural, normal fear. This phenomenon stems from the demand for complete control of their environment. Should an unexpected or frightening situation arise, the reaction will be anger rather than the more natural response of fear. They will appear to be in control even in the most out of control situation. To a well-trained host of an Anger-based control spirit, fear is not an option.

Several years before my wife's deliverance, she brought pizza home for the family. We were pastoring in a small town and living in the parsonage. On pizza night, we would rent a movie and eat our pizza while sitting around the television. This particular evening, we each grabbed our slices from the box and rushed into the family room for the start of the movie. Upon sitting down, we heard my wife coming. She was fuming. She marched into the room, swiped every slice off our plates and slammed them back into the box.

Then, out the door she flew.

We heard the rest of this story later from stunned onlookers. She dashed back to the pizza shop and called the very tall, rather large manager out to the register. She went up one side of him and down the other. She told him where to get off and how she was going to make his life miserable. The poor man never knew what hit him. My little five-foot tall wife—all of a hundred and fifteen pounds soaking wet—nearly made the big brute cry right there in front of God and everybody. The result was they put Mrs. Mather's name on the wall of the pizza shop so anytime she called in an order she was afforded pizza with more cheese on it than you could imagine.

You see, when it came time for her to take her piece of pizza, there was pizza left, but no cheese, you know, pizza sixteen inches across with a little circle of cheese in the middle maybe ten inches across. Would you lose your mind over it? Probably not. But she could not stand to be cheated. That meant someone had abused her. She wouldn't have that. Her response was an enormous overreaction. As we have learned: victims always victimize, and certainly, those carrying an anger based control spirit will be experts at it.

Although, sometimes I miss that pizza . . .

The Method of Manipulation

The modus operandi of the Anger-based control spirit is simple: the resident natural anger the host experienced within the parameters of the trauma or as a natural part of his/her family line is amplified until it becomes a frenetic, unmanageable monster. Though excessive anger is a lack of control opposing the mission of the unclean spirit, the host will justify such action, finding security in the expulsion of anger. His/her paradigm will be formed to make room for these outbursts in the pursuit of equilibrium in his/her life. As a result, those around the victim will submit to the authority of the controller to keep peace in the relationship. The host will then be free to exercise whatever authority he/she wants, and those connected with him/her will do anything he/she asks to avoid being the target of his/her anger. He/she will be able to manipulate people and circumstances to his/her own advantage and move himself/herself into higher levels of authority with ease.

The manipulative part of it all is that the host will probably be utterly unaware any other force is at work in the situation. He/she will be content with his/her exercise of authority because he/she will be convinced everyone will benefit from what is being done.

THE MODE OF CONTROL

Anger is the first in the list of control spirits that can cause the person to be extremely domineering. The power of the anger released causes the target to cower, back down and abdicate authority. The husband of a woman hosting an Anger-based control spirit will learn early in the marriage that the punishment he receives is never worth whatever infraction of the rules he intended to commit. The anger she feels and expresses is more than can be conjured up in her natural mind and heart. It is empowered and then multiplied as it is expelled.

Children growing up under an Anger-based control spirit parent will fall into one of two distinct categories. One may carry the next generation of the Anger-based control spirit and will fight fire with fire. These kids will not be able to wait until they get out of high school to flee the house and set up their own reign of terror. Many leave home early. Others fight their way through, driven towards perfection, and die early from heart attacks trying to prove themselves worthy of their parent's approval.

Still others crumble under the constant barrage of anger. They spend their time fixing and cleaning up messes--physical, emotional and relational messes--so the control spirit will remain hidden from view. This spirit resident in parents is the manufacturer of weak, broken people who never seem to find their niche in life. The domineering mother, perhaps manifesting a control spirit, is one prime cause of emasculated boys developing effeminacy and then escaping into a homosexual lifestyle. Domineering fathers are the cause of destroyed girls who are unable to form proper relationships and frequently choose men very much like their own controlling father to marry. It is astonishing how many emotionally, physically, and verbally battered girls turn out to be battered wives, unable to summon the courage to escape the prison of abuse.

LIKELY DOORWAY FOR DEMONIZATION

As we've said before, the most frequent cause of this type of demonization in women is sexual abuse. Several years ago, we came across a statistic stating one out of three adult women have been sexually abused before the age of eighteen.[8] The accompanying numbers for men were equally startling. The study found that one in five adult men had been sexually abused before the age of eighteen. Dr. Dan Allender, author of *The Wounded Heart*, shared in a seminar that he believes the percentage of sexual abuse victims is as high as eighty-five percent in society as well as in the Church.[9]

This understanding provides insight into the level of demonization in the culture and further, in the Church. These damaged people are pressing into the Church to find healing and peace but, by and large, the Church has failed them. The doorway for their torment is seldom closed because the Church has civilized deliverance out of their programs. The very antidote for what ails humanity has been pick-pocketed by the forces of evil.

The Path To Wholeness

The recovery time for those finding freedom from an Anger-based control spirit is difficult to predict. The learned behavior is so interwoven into their being so as to require an all-out pursuit of Father, a heavy dose of counseling, and a fierce determination to pull it off. The focus of this pursuit must be to allow the Lord to expose the anger sources and to concentrate on discovering a proper expression of anger.

The course of action Father usually takes is frequently contrary to what the client might expect. Rather than sheltering the person from situations that would normally cause anger, Father tends to create more of them while pressing the recoveree right into the fray. It seems He uses a sort of on-the-job-training to bring the person to wholeness while building up his/her power to withstand the learned behavior. As much as we warn them of the impending struggle, they continue to hold onto the hope of being cocooned until it is all over. They expect to immediately emerge whole and free from the issues that created the problem in the first place.

The length of time required to press the recoveree through varies with the person. However, one must remember that he/she did not get that way in a day; therefore, it will take more than a day to come out from the years of learned behavior which always accompanies demonization. The only way to move through it is to get started, and then stay motivated and focused upon the goal of healing and wholeness. We encourage the recovering person to embrace the painful process rather than run from it. The tenacity demonstrated by the recoveree is always the deciding factor for both the length of recovery time and the extent to which he/she fully recovers and lives abundantly.

The wholeness process is simply the necessary expenditure of time and energy in transitioning from life in darkness and bondage into life in the light. In as much as the outcome is wonderful, there is a sense in which the process is difficult and often painful as parts of the victim are cut away and put to death in favor of an alien Presence taking up residence in its place. It is the definition of the process of *"work[ing] out your salvation with fear and trembling, for it is God who works in you to will and to act according to his good purpose"* (Philippians 2:12-13). One pastor's wife remarked that undergoing deliverance was "like being born again all over again."[10] She is right, in that, deliverance is an integral part of the work of the Cross. Since she had been born again for many years prior to her deliverance experience, to receive the rest of the story of salvation was simply the conclusion to the process she had begun so long ago. With her new freedom in hand, she is able to discover the true liberty of life in the Kingdom of Light.

Chapter 8

FEAR-BASED CONTROL SPIRITS

A Spirit of Fear

Another basic type of control spirit is the Fear-based control spirit. The probable response to the trauma that provided the doorway for demonization was to be overcome by fear. Again, it must be understood that the doorway, in this case *fear*, comes first, and then the demon, waiting like a vulture, preys upon the person. Fear takes root in the person and becomes a place of darkness into which the demon may be introduced.

The presence of a spirit of fear (II Timothy 1:7) does not necessarily indicate a Fear-based control spirit. There are ordinary spirits of fear that consume and harass people. However, the presence of a Fear-based control spirit is a significant leap in authority, power, devastation, and manipulation. Where a spirit of fear might torment its host, the Fear-based control spirit takes it to the next level. While tormenting its host it also torments those in relationship with the host, controlling them, manipulating them, and even attempting to develop a doorway in them for the entrance of their own spirit of fear.

Most fears, unnatural and natural, may be demonically multiplied. We have seen many diagnosed phobias cured through deliverance and the subsequent walking out of the wholeness process. One client is of particular interest. We will call her Carol. Carol was unable to leave her house. She was being treated for several phobias, not the least of which was agoraphobia: the fear of public places or open spaces. If she had to go to the mall, the walk through the expansive hallways would cripple her. Therefore, she had not been there in years. In addition, she had a fear of crowds, so she was unable to handle sitting through a church service. When we conducted her deliverance session, the unclean spirit was revealed as a ruler level spirit, a Fear-based control spirit. During the session, the spirit levitated her and moved her toward the door in an attempt to get her out of the room and avoid being cast out. We quickly positioned a team member between her and the door and were able to see Carol set free. Since that time, she has been thrilled to worship with the saints and she has a love of shopping, which, instead of causing *her* to fear, frightens her husband.

THE METHOD OF MANIPULATION

This fear manipulates the victim, but it is primarily used to manipulate those around him/her. By exhibiting fear, he/she can induce people to serve him/her and do what he/she wants them to do. By introducing a higher-level fear into situations, the control spirit can control the course of organizations such as churches, or even towns and cities. Manipulation is the tool and hindrance is the goal.

Often, those manipulated by a Fear-based control spirit are afraid of everything. Some may be able to mask some of their fear, but most are completely ruled by it. They will fear small and great things alike. This spirit will be exposed every time there is opportunity for anxiety.

Alice's greatest fear was about to be realized: her son was going to kindergarten. During the week leading up to the fateful day she spent nearly every night sleepless and anxious, looking for a way to make it all go away. Instead of Teddy weeping at the door of the classroom as he entered for the first time, it was his Mom standing there shaking, tears streaming down her face. Her inner turmoil overwhelmed her. He was nauseous and disoriented. She spent the next few years driven by her fears, transmitting those fears to her son. The fear, now ruling every aspect of her son's life, created the weak area necessary for his own demonization. As she overwhelmed and dominated him through her fears, his spirit was crushed and he, like so many others in our culture, succumbed to a homosexual spirit and is living that lifestyle today.

A Fear-based control spirit in a parent will frequently be transmitted as a familiar spirit to the children. Just as the child may have his mother's eyes, or looks just like his uncle Fred, so the generational curse of the parent's spiritual life will be passed down from generation to generation.

Randy came to our ministry a very sick man. He was allergic to everything. He packed bottles of pills and other paraphernalia to manage his allergies. He was allergic to dust and suffered under chronic sinus infections. He was unable to eat certain foods, be exposed to certain chemicals and could not really enjoy the outdoors for any length of time without succumbing to some allergic attack. As a result of his illnesses, he was kept from any sort of athletics or other strenuous activity for fear of an attack. His mother hovered over him, restricting his movements and speaking fear into his ears.

In his deliverance session, it became clear his mother was the domineering influence in his life and had created her son in her own image. She was afraid his sniffles were the preamble to pneumonia or some terminal condition. She was sure that if he played with other children he would be maimed in a horrible accident. Her anxiety was overwhelming and all-powerful. "It's all fun and games until someone's eye gets poked out" was the ruling force of her life.

In the years following his deliverance, Randy has pursued

Father with passion and has had very few sinus infections since. He abandoned his pill case and is living free from his allergies. Now the question is: "Was he delivered or healed; or did he just choose not to be a hypochondriac like his mother had instilled into him?" To be frank, it does not really matter, as long as he is set free from the bondage. However, it most likely is a combination of all three. Jesus said, *"The truth will set you free"* (John 8:32) and it is as true today as it was then. When the truth is prophetically revealed in a deliverance session, that truth will be the driving force for freedom from the bondage once ruling the person's life. The most important portion of Randy's session was the breaking of the powerful generational curse line handed down to him from his mother.

A healthy fear is necessary for proper worship. *"The fear of the Lord is the beginning of knowledge"* (Proverbs 1:7). Most of the time, the only fear we experience within our Christian walk is the fear of demons and the dark kingdom. For most modern Christians, the thought of a demon appearing evokes great fear, while the thought of Father showing up causes nothing of the sort. In the wholeness process, Father will assist the victim of unnatural fears find a proper healthy usage of fear: the awed respect of the Living God. Fear, then, is the highest of priority for Satan and his minions as he attempts to step into the place of Father and be feared.

THE EXTERNAL WORKINGS

Because fear is so much a part of the natural state of mankind in our Godless condition, it is fairly easy to understand how one may be controlled by it internally. When the Fear-based control spirit is present, the external machinery comes on line and fear spreads to those around the host. A netherworld of fear is created out of which there appears to be no escape.

Sally's mom was afraid. She was probably afraid of a lot of things, but her greatest fear was the fear of embarrassment. She spent the bulk of her time harping to her children about how the house looked to others, how the wash should not be left on the clothesline too long, after all, "We don't want the neighbors to think we're the Beverly Hillbillies." This fear was rehearsed constantly--never let them see your weakness-until the children began taking on the phobias associated with it. They became perfectionistic and obsessive about what people thought about them.

Sally became her mother.

Now, Sally's fear of people's opinions drove her to try to please them, to see they did not think any bad thoughts about her or her family. She worked constantly to achieve the approval of those around her, while her immediate family was neglected. She must dress herself and her family properly for fear of what others might think. She must have the right house, the right car, the right husband and the right children. Of course, the pitfall is easily seen: nothing was ever right enough. She drove herself physically, mentally and emotionally until she began to break down. Over time, she regularly experienced nervous breakdowns and her marriage was held together by a thread. Her children exhibited the same neurotic tendencies she experienced as a child. Her husband treaded on eggshells.

She needed relief.

She came to us for deliverance and was set free from the demonic multiplication of her fears. Then, she set her mind toward healing the learned behavior and sealing the breaches in her beliefs that allowed the infestation to rule her. Today, she is healing nicely. Her children are learning to like her. They have undergone deliverance as well. When they drive her to the brink, she has found a marvelous way to cope. She says, "I just remember that my children were raised by demons." Her husband received deliverance also and is loving Sally through her journey to wholeness.

Worry

The worrier is a professional in the realm of fear. One who worries exercises enormous control over those about whom they are anxious. It masquerades as an act of love and concern to worry about someone, however, the simple act of expressing, "I am so worried about you" displays the worrier's need to feel safe about the circumstances. Once it is expressed, the person who is worried over must supply the worrier with a proper response.

There are only two ways to respond to worry. First, it can be ignored. Of course, this is the dangerous approach. The worrier's response to being ignored will be to heighten the worry to a whirlwind until it cannot be ignored. Many times, this will be manifest in a nervous breakdown, some sort of mental or physical collapse, or sudden emergence or reemergence of an illness powerful enough to force the person ignoring the worry to capitulate and submit to the rule of the worrier. The only other alternative is going right to the last step and let the worrier control you or the situation. Children who grow up under such rule have learned to avoid the argument and to facilitate the fear of the worrier as soon as possible. For the most part, husbands of the professional worrier develop selective hearing loss. They trek through life apparently oblivious to the impending devastation expected by their anxious spouse.

The Journey To Wholeness

The path toward wholeness for a former host of a Fear-based control spirit is an adventure. Since fear out of balance and improperly aimed is bondage, the path to wholeness will require the person to jump out right into the middle of those things that formerly controlled them and let go of the safety mechanisms they had created to make them feel safe. As with all control spirits, the presence of the unclean spirit is difficult to see because its modus operandi is to make the fearful person feel safe. Its presence therefore creates an illusion of security and comfort instead of revealing it to be the source of the fear. Though it uses fear against the person, the control comes from its duplicitous nature. The unclean spirit will use the natural fears of the person, multiply them until they are completely out of control, and then feign coming along side to comfort the person, by turning the fear around and directing it outward. This routine becomes the safety mechanism for the victim and makes him/her feel in control of an out-of-control situation.

As wholeness is pursued, Father will insure that the recoveree will be faced with one fearful situation after another so that he/she may practice walking out the experience with confidence and without turning the control mechanism outward. Mary is a wonderful example. One of her multitude of fears was the fear of flying. Once through deliverance and into her wholeness process, Father clearly indicated that she and her husband travel with us to perform deliverances in our conferences. Father pressed her into the very place of fear so that He could show her His kindness in healing her. Chris and Mary are beginning to build up frequent flyer miles.

Wholeness, while sounding like a wonderful thing, is truly found on the other side of a great chasm. In the chasm can be found everything that causes fear, worry, confusion, and anxiety. The responsibility of the recoveree "is to understand who [they] are and, with help of Jesus Christ, become free of any damaging results from our past."[11] Herein might be the simple approach to understanding the wholeness process: Father, in His wisdom, simply pushes our fear buttons until we no longer respond to them or allow them to have control over us and thereby cause us to attempt to control others. It may appear cruel for the Lord to allow fearful situations to happen, but His desire is we would leave our old responses and look to Him for a revelation of new responses based in His provision for us.

Chapter 9

MARTYR-BASED CONTROL SPIRITS

WEAK AND MEEK

Perhaps the most difficult control spirit to understand is the Martyr-based control spirit. The host of such a spirit will most likely appear to be the farthest possible thing from a controller. In fact, one of the most common characteristics of someone carrying this type of spirit is he/she is a pitiful or a pitiable person. Whereas the other types of control spirits are often strong, forceful and demanding, our martyr must be understood as the antithesis. His or her power will materialize out of weakness.

These characteristics are the greatest weapons of the Martyr-based control spirit.

OH, WOE IS ME

The host of a Martyr-based control spirit generally has such a low self-image that he/she will readily sacrifice personal comforts for others. These sacrifices are the only place in which any personal value may be found. Frequently, it is only within this purview of self-sacrifice that he/she feels acceptable. Of course, this feeling must be previously resident in the person before an unclean spirit can inhabit it. Then, they are manipulated by the unclean spirit in a manner that multiplies the effects of the low self-esteem into the dominating force of his/her existence.

Once again, this is the agenda of demonization: to take a tiny seed and make it the greatest tree in the garden. Demons never create anything. Instead, they squat on a dark place in our being—a place of damage or sin—inhabit it, and cultivate their influence until it becomes the defining portion of our personality. This is one of the main reasons why psychologists and psychiatrists cannot cure what are defined as mental illnesses. They are relegated to managing the consequences of the damage, medicating it, and helping the person talk about it for years, sometimes decades, without really healing the person.

However, through deliverance, the victim who has been inhabited by an unclean spirit may find a complete cure. An extended timeframe is likely required, but healing is the normal result of the deliverance and wholeness process. We have extensive experience with recoverees from Martyr-based control spirits and find them to be pleasant, joyous men and women of God once the first few years of their journey to wholeness have been successfully navigated.

The Method of Manipulation

Hosts of Martyr-based control spirits manipulate their prey by guilt. Guilt is obviously one of the strongest forces in the human manipulation arsenal. "You don't have to buy me anything" should be written into a tear-jerking, whiny country Christmas carol for all the martyrs among us. These people see themselves as unlovable and therefore unworthy of any act of love. This creates a dichotomy in their lives: they cannot receive love while they, at the same moment, are desperate to be loved. Since they are unlovable, the only type of love they are willing to accept is the love they manipulate others to give them. Over time, a hidden anger may develop that remains deeply embedded in the recesses of the heart, forming the very fabric of their existence.

The hosts will seldom, if ever, let their anger escape, so it will fester unchecked. This internal conflagration will likely result in some physical manifestation such as cancer or some other incurable disease often characterized by a rotting from the inside out.

If you are sensing confusion in this logic, you have found the real power of the Martyr-based control spirit. She will not allow others to love her, all the while demanding attention through the use of Martyr language. The ever-present mother who cannot sit down and eat with the family because she is caught up in serving the holiday meal is a classic example. She does for others until she cannot stand, while refusing help to make the load lighter. This is an obvious cry for help. She has so given into the lie of the control spirit that her identity is found in the sacrifice. Without it, she is lost. She is unable to sit by while others serve her because she can only find love and affection in the doing. Her character is therefore defined by the martyrdom.

Another typical example is the pastor who does everything for the sheep of his congregation, working himself into exhaustion—bags under his eyes and all—while refusing to allow the workload to be lightened by the sheep. This is definitely a control issue he uses to make himself indispensable to those he serves. In return, he asks nothing, not to their faces, that is. He finds great spirituality in suffering alone for the sake of the sheep. The process begins with pure motives. However, his heart will eventually succumb to bitterness toward those he serves.

Should any of the sheep choose to leave him, his response will first be a pathetic plea for them to stay. Should they not yield to this tactic, he will extend to them some position within the scope of his ministry beyond their current level of authority or maturity as an enticement for their continued loyalty. When this fails, he will lash out at them with a vicious attack, leaving them flabbergasted at his savagery. This final blow is often dealt through a letter instead of face-to-face, since his insecurities utterly rule him. "Spiritually abusive systems are easy to get into but hard to leave. The leaders assume power and demand obedience. They foster loyalty to the organization with implied or covert scare tactics and threats."12 Everything for this pastor is about controlling the sheep and keeping them in check. His martyr behavior elevates himself to "savior of the sheep," replacing the Good Shepherd with an inferior replica.

The Mode of Control

In the apparent self-sacrificing action there is concealed an expectation. He expects others to stop what they are doing, giving him their rapt attention. He assumes they now owe him for his sacrifice. He anticipates others will have pity on him and to do what he wants them to do. This system of owing favors is the core of the Martyr-based control spirit's scheme. When others do something for him without provocation, he will be genuinely upset and will not receive even well motivated attention. Instead, he must control them through making them owe him.

He will find it intolerable to owe someone else, and will likely take the appropriate action immediately to settle the debt, how ever small it may seem to the receiver. If he owes something to someone, he will interpret the situation as being under the control of the other person, which cannot be tolerated. This unmasks the core lie of the control spirit: love is a commodity used to control rather than a gift to be celebrated and shared. He will only understand that, unless others feel guilty enough to owe him attention, affection and love, no one loves him. He will repel any attempt to freely love him. He will despise anyone who loves him easily, rejecting the love out-of-hand. His fear of being unloved drives him to be an unlovable person.

The Pitiful Hypochondriac

The Martyr-based control spirit's arsenal is full of schemes manipulating the health of the host. What better means of exacting sympathy than being chronically ill? When a person is in and out of the hospital, forever seeing the doctor for another prescription, persistently ailing with one incurable or rare malady or another, those close to them are automatically expected to pay through obligatory visits, gifts and pity.

It must be noted that we are an ailing society and there are many truly sick and diseased among us. This section does not apply in those cases. This is a lifelong pattern of manipulation and is not reserved for the elderly or infirm. Do not allow guilt to overcome you should the remainder of the conditions required to diagnose a Martyr-based control spirit be present.

I once witnessed a miraculous healing. The woman had suffered with Multiple Sclerosis for many years until she was relegated to a wheelchair for what remained of her life. When the man of God prayed for her, she stood up and began running around the church. It was all very thrilling and astonishing. However, within a very few months she relapsed and once again found herself in her wheelchair. There was much speculation as to her lack of faith; certainly she must have been living in secret sin to return to her handicap so quickly. Surely, the Lord was punishing her.

Months later, the truth of the matter was discovered. She confessed that when her wheelchair was no longer needed, she immediately lost the special attention she loved. She had needed help in coming to church, people always greeted her in a special way, she had the attention of a personal nurse, and the attention of anyone around her while she sat in the wheelchair. When the chair was gone, and she became "normal" she was afforded none of that special attention. She could get from place to place without help; she could open the door and walk through it without any assistance; and she merited no special treatment.

The Martyr-based control spirit had inhabited the weak area of her life and she had manipulated people for her own pleasure.

After the healing, she chose to return to the chair so that she could control the people around her and draw sympathy for herself and the miracle was negated by the manipulation of the unclean spirit. She passed away having never walked again.

THE LIKELY DOORWAY FOR DEMONIZATION

As is the case with the majority of women hosting control spirits, a person infected by a Martyr-based control spirit probably will have been the victim of childhood sexual abuse. As we have seen, sexual abuse creates a sense of powerlessness affecting "all aspects of the victim's life."[13] This type of trauma produces enough darkness within him/her to survive the salvation experience and yet remain the ruling factor of life. She will, when challenged, explain that she has always been this way; it is just her personality. A damaged personality is the doorway for most demonization; her personality must be changed through walking out the path to wholeness. As she finds greater levels of freedom and liberty, the personality change will emerge.

Another doorway for this type of demonic influence is neglect. The neglect may have been as ostensibly benign as being born a middle child in the family or as ghastly as parental abandonment. When such trauma occurs, the victim, whose response is self-pity, will likely be fertile ground for a Martyr-based control spirit. The person who reacts with anger may be fertile ground for an Anger-based control spirit. The person whose response is fear may be an open target for a Fear-based control spirit. Based upon the nature and personality of the victim, unclean spirits will prey upon the weak place and use that weakness as the means for control.

Additionally, we have found another doorway may be sickness. When a child is sickly, he/she feels a sense of isolation and fear that is only allayed by the attention of the medical community and his/her family as they express pity for his/her condition. A sickly child will be trained to know that the sicker he/she is, the more attention he/she is apt to receive. Even when the sickness is long-passed in his/her physical body, his/her emotions may be permanently educated in the power of manipulation. This is an open door for demonization.

It is obvious that we are discussing a young person with an immature worldview. However, since we adults are a compilation of our entire life experience, the damaged place remains a foothold of darkness throughout our lives and may be used as an unconscious defense mechanism against the fear of rejection. Because these damaged emotions have been left intact, unchallenged and in control of the balance of our lives, we simply assume: "That's just who I am." Our personality is blamed for our dysfunction. Therefore, when demonization occurs, we remain unaware of its presence or power to rule us, and then we continue to be the children we were.

THE PATH TO WHOLENESS

The host of a Martyr-based control spirit will find recovery to be difficult at best and excruciating at worst. Because the influence of this spirit is so covert, the authenticity of its absence will be hard to document. As with most other types of control spirit, the host is rarely aware of its presence. Once it becomes clear that the unclean spirit is resident and deliverance occurs, the initial stages of recovery must focus upon discovering how the spirit manipulated both the host and the people around him/her.

We have heard the following question many times: "Does this mean I was just a horrid person and that everyone around me suffered from my very presence?" One problem with deliverance and wholeness ministry is we must be dedicated to telling the truth. This may seem odd, but we are convinced that within the traditional church structure people rarely tell you the truth. In the recovery process, the maxim "the truth hurts" becomes an every day verity. The answer to the above question is, "Yes."

Of course, we are quick to add that it all will change with the pursuit of Father in the wholeness process.

The recovery will be slow at first. The recoveree should join a small group in which safety and accountability may be found. Should he/she be married, the spouse must be instructed in his/her role for assisting the recovery. For a wife bound by a spirit of control, greater levels of healing will come through the participation of her husband. For a husband, it may require the intervention of a strong male counterpart to reach the highest level of healing.

Whatever the case, the victim of the Martyr-based control spirit will need to be encouraged constantly. Because the doorway for the demonization is tied to low self-esteem and self-loathing, the recoveree will require constant observation to keep him/her from falling into despair and self-pity. Many have expressed the need to stop the process simply because they do not think they are worth the effort. This must be revealed for exactly what is it: selfishness. The host of the Martyr-based control spirit is simply expressing enormous selfishness. To find healing, this person must recognize and relinquish the root causes of selfishness and allow Christ to reconstruct a Biblical self-view. Good Christian recovery material such as Robert McGee's *The Search For Significance* is essential to acquire a balanced self view out of which the healing can manifest.

Chapter 10

PLEASER-BASED CONTROL SPIRITS

THE UPSIDE-DOWN CONTROL SPIRIT

The Pleaser-based control spirit manipulates its victims through doing all sorts of wonderful things for its prey in order to get him/her to comply with its demands. This will often appear as the total opposite of what a control spirit should be. Nevertheless, the host of a Pleaser-based spirit will control their surroundings with equal power and authority as an Anger-based control spirit.

For many years, we identified this demon as an upside-down control spirit. Its behavior and method of control were in complete contrast from a typical control spirit. This spirit may best be described as a spirit of 'nice.' It motivates its host to perform all sorts of charitable deeds or acts of kindness in order to ingratiate the target of the manipulation. Once the target receives one or more of these benevolent actions, a sense of obligation is created toward the host of the spirit. However, the target is frequently unaware of the manipulation and will register no sense of alarm even as the noose is tightened around his/her neck. This is why the Pleaser-based control spirit is so insidious. Rather than feeling degraded or used by the host of this unclean spirit, the target of the control will usually feel quite satisfied about the transaction.

The Politician

The Pleaser-based control spirit is a politician. As instructed by the demon, the host tells the target anything he/she thinks he wants to hear and will do whatever is necessary in order to secure whatever control he/she is craving. This craving can manifest in any number of ways. He/she may be craving friendship and will do whatever he/she thinks the target desires to obligate him to spend time with her. He/she may be feeling powerless, and thus will perform some act of kindness so one is obliged to capitulate to his/her in a specific situation. In some cases, the motivation is simply that the host cannot say "No" to anyone because he/she cannot allow anyone to feel unhappy.

Whatever the case, the motivation is often apparently benign. It will seldom directly threaten the host, nor will it openly parade its true intentions. Instead, at least in the beginning of the relationship, the target may be pleased by the "go to guy" he has discovered. It is only when reciprocal demands are made that the target will find out the truth.

The technique of this unclean spirit is the epitome of the deal making that goes on between politicians. The pleaser will make the target happy only to coerce him into conforming to the host's wishes. The subtlety is deceptive because one is made to feel good by the apparent act of kindness precipitating the exercise of control.

What Can I Do To Make You Happy

Dr. Kevin Leman, in his book, *The Pleasers*, identifies the fertile ground in the personality into which the demonic influence may penetrate. He classifies six major characteristics of the pleaser personality.[14] These women learned to be pleasers when they were little girls. Pleasers often come from unhappy homes in which their fathers gave them very little attention, support, or love. Pleasers are willing to settle for small favors. And that brings us to perhaps the key characteristic in almost all pleasers: low self-esteem. A strong characteristic of pleasers is trying to keep everyone happy. Pleasers usually feel inferior to men, or at least have a strong need to be "good girls" so men will approve of them.

These personality characteristics do not necessarily indicate the presence of demonic influence. However, they certainly provide clues to the source of the demonization, should that be the diagnosis. When there is found to be demonic infestation, the above characteristics are always found to be present.

Louise was a classic example of someone hosting a Pleaser-based control spirit. She was a social butterfly and everyone thought she was wonderful. Every move she made appeared to be selfless and aimed at making those around her happy. She picked up the check at dinner so the rest of the evening would be under her control. She put her children on display to make people think well of her as a mother. She seemed to be the perfect wife and people hailed her for her wonderful family. She cared for people, going out of her way to make them happy. She appeared to have it all together. However, in the privacy of her own home, she neglected the children, despised her husband and spent most of her time sullen and lonely.

Her life was out of control.

She had been sexually abused when she was a child, resulting in deep insecurities. Those insecurities, combined with her particular personality, allowed her to be besieged by an unclean spirit who ostensibly demonstrated the way to keep her life under control. She developed the coping mechanisms, under the influence of the inhabiting Pleaser-based control spirit, whereby she would preemptively attempt to please those who intimidated her or made her afraid. The rationale was likely along the lines of "if you make them happy, they will not hurt you." Therefore, the outward evidence of the presence of a control spirit seldom appeared to be an act of control. On the contrary, Louise gave the impression of not controlling at all.

Louise was unable to say "No" to anyone. If asked to inconvenience herself for someone, she would make the necessary arrangements to ensure the other person was not unhappy. Consequently, the only way Louise could feel safe and secure was to make sure no one was unhappy. In this frenzied existence she found protection and her life was apparently under control. Her "obsessing, controlling, obsessive 'helping,' low self-worth bordering on self-hatred, self-repression, [and] abundance of anger and guilt"[15] drove her constantly, never allowing her to rest and enjoy her life.

Her family suffered the effects of the control spirit in fairly typical ways. The pool man shared his unhappiness with Louise on several occasions. Her internal response was fear and insecurity, so she had to make him happy in order for her to feel safe. She took care of his loneliness at the expense of her marriage.

The children, paraded perfectly dressed and cute in public, were only a minor inconvenience back at home. They were left to raise themselves as mom flitted about caring for the needs of those who could reciprocate adequately and make her feel safe. As with all control spirit situations, there are casualties. In this case, the children were sacrificed upon the altar of control.

THE LIFE OF THE PLEASER

The public persona of a host of a Pleaser-based control spirit will almost always appear upbeat and positive. This "can do" attitude is the foundation for his/her existence. If the target needs a certain thing or is uncertain in a situation, the host of this unclean spirit will be well trained in moving in and fixing whatever is amiss. The obvious result of such action is that the one helped is grateful for the positive outcome of his/her problem. The next step in this process is the demand for a reciprocal action by the target for the host. The host will manipulate the target into doing something and the target will be obligated to do it whether or not he wants to do it. In time, the target of such control may become aware of the manipulation and may become bitter toward the host. Frequently, by the time this awareness occurs, the target will be so indebted to the host of the Pleaser-based control spirit that it becomes impossible to say "No" or to break the grip in which he finds himself. This will inevitably lead to one of two things: either the target will sever the relationship, or will keep quiet, permanently succumbing to the control of the host.

Should their target break away, the hosts, probably unaware any control has been exercised at all, will be confused and hurt by such a violent response. We have found that hosts are so engrossed in denial they seldom understand either the response of the target breaking away or the reality of their own actions. As with all control spirits, the Pleaser-based control spirit will educate its host in such a way as to control people and situations without conscious awareness of what they are actually doing. Consequently, it is nearly impossible to convince them of their demonization prior to the deliverance session. Many hosts of Pleaser-based control spirits have agreed to submit to deliverance because they think it will make someone within their relationship circle happy. However, the majority of them do so sincerely, thus they are in the position to be set free from something they did not even know was holding them captive.

These hosts will seldom reveal weakness unless it serves to please the target of their control. We have witnessed the host of a Pleaser-based control spirit make the target happy by allowing them to provide a solution to a problem from which the host was suffering. In this way, the host gained sympathy from the helper, which was used to obtain relationship. The fact that the friendship is based upon an illusion does not seem to concern the host. His/her only concern is his/her own sense of security.

Although the host of a Pleaser-based control spirit may appear to have it all together, his/her life will be characterized by hollowness. There is an emptiness within the core of the pleaser. The unclean spirit will, in its attempts to mollify everyone in its sphere of influence, devour the host. Over time, the host of a Pleaser-based control spirit will become more and more hollow. If he/she could be transparent, he/she would reveal a sense of emptiness regarding every area of life.

Since they remain in such a state of denial about their own life, depression and self-pity are seldom options. The Pleaser-based spirit will repair any such weaknesses by ensuring the presence of someone who needs to be fixed. Therefore, the life of the hosts will be fixed by fixing others. Unless someone can break through this wall of denial and help the pleasers find the truth, they will continue being devoured from the inside out, living out life in emptiness and loneliness, running from one person to the other, making each as happy as possible.

THE MALE OF THE SPECIES

It seemed as though George was never home. He was an electrician by trade and worked for a large utilities company who kept him very busy. He worked a regular forty-hour workweek and was on call every other weekend running down electrical problems that cropped up across the service area. This life suited him, and he and his family appeared happy.

But, everyone has electrical problems in their homes. They need an outlet here; they need additional circuit breakers to handle the load of their new appliances; or they want to put in a new, larger service to meet the revised electrical codes. And nobody knows very much about electrical issues.

Except, of course, for George.

Everyone was unhappy with their electrical problems, so they called George. At first, it might be just to ask a question, but soon, George was constrained to stop by and solve their problems, making them happy and meeting his inner compulsion to keep the world safe from unhappiness. Most nights of the week, George would arrive home from work, quickly eat his dinner, only to head right back out the door to rescue someone else from his electrical unhappiness.

Obviously, George's family seldom spent time with him. Even when he was not saving someone else, the insecurities of his life drove him to undertake continuous projects for his home that kept him out of contact with them even while he was actually at home. He worked so hard at keeping his reputation for being a workaholic, he had little energy left to spend any quality time with his kids. Consequently, his kids were terrors--undisciplined and self-absorbed. No one wanted to baby-sit or invite them over for fear of the children. This condition was the result of George's inability to see them unhappy. When they should have been disciplined, he would ignore them rather than make them unhappy through loving discipline. He also refused to interact with his wife. He could not confront her, so, even though she was a wonderful woman, he chose to disappear into his work rather than to be put in the position either to confront or to be confronted.

Then, George came to us for deliverance. We identified and dismissed the Pleaser-based control spirit in a matter of minutes. However, his recovery period was not as effortless. In working through his issues with his wife, he discovered the source of his demonization to be the divorce of his parents and the subsequent disappearance of his mother. He had been about five years old and could not process the fact that his mom abandoned him. We discovered that his emotions arrested at that moment and he had not grown an inch emotionally from then until his deliverance. He was now in his mid thirties physically while remaining about five years old emotionally. The trauma imposed by his mother's departure left him an emotional cripple. The revelation came clear: as a five year old, he had thought that his mom left because she was unhappy with him. The rest of George's life, unbeknownst to him, was devoted to making people happy in order to keep himself safe. With the introduction of the unclean spirit into his life, this condition was compounded until it controlled not only him, but also everyone and everything in his life. "This type of boundary problem paralyzes people's no muscles. Whenever they need to protect themselves by saying no, the word catches in their throats."[16]

His recovery extended for several years. He was required to grow up in the arrested areas of his life. The pain was excruciating. Everything he thought he understood about the world and how it works was suspect. He was able to kindly decline invitations to save people from themselves electrically. He found himself able to withstand the insecurities of raising his children and dared to make them unhappy by telling them "No" when appropriate. George was finally able to set the proper boundaries for his life and work.

His kids have made a remarkable recovery as well. They have become delightful people, disciplined and well adjusted. His wife has become a new woman in conjunction with his growth into an emotionally mature man. George stays at home more, is intimately involved in the affairs of his household, and now serves Father because he desires to do so instead of out of compulsion.

Though the Pleaser-based control spirit may seem benign, the effects for this family, as well as many others, are devastating.

Chapter 11

SEX-BASED CONTROL SPIRITS

SEXUAL ABUSE VICTIMS

Another type of control spirit is the Sex-based control spirit. This spirit primarily attaches itself to a person who has experienced some sort of sexual abuse. Since, as we have already pointed out, the statistics reveal that approximately one in three adult women, and one in five men have experienced sexual abuse before the age of eighteen, the odds are very high that people carrying this kind of spirit are in the Church seeking help. Such abuse always causes damage severe enough to provide fertile ground for demonization.

The trauma induced by a sexual predator upon an unsuspecting, unwilling victim--one who does not understand or have the mental capacity to willingly participate, that is, being too young to understand--permanently damages the emotions and paradigms of the victim. As indicted by Sandra Brown in her book about treating victims of violence, "The magnitude of psychological problems that sexual abuse causes for children is vast."[17] The fundamental consequence of such damage is the victim will acquire an excessive fear of being out of control. In his/her attempt to bring life back under control, coping mechanisms are developed to maintain a safe and protected environment. Though these may begin in the psyche of the victim, demons will attack like vultures to compound the effects and inhabit these coping mechanisms. They will then provide security in exchange for demonic rulership. Instead of healing, the trauma continues as the centerpiece of the victim's existence for a lifetime.

Two Roads Diverge

Once a demon inhabits the dark place provided by the trauma, the eventual product takes one of two basic forms. The first response is to press the victim into sexually abusing others before they have the opportunity to be sexually abused. The subconscious rule is: the abuser has the power. Therefore, the victim will learn to abuse first before being abused, thus gaining power over those who would potentially bring him/her harm. The victim of sexual abuse may choose to enter into sexual situations willingly and aggressively in order to maintain control of the situation. They may choose multiple partners over a lifetime, unable, for any significant length of time, to remain monogamous.

One common response that has come into vogue in recent history is to move into lesbianism, cutting the abusing male of the species entirely out of the equation. Within the lesbian relationship the victims find security from sexually aggressive men. However, they are still living in promiscuity within this type of relationship and continue victimizing themselves and their partner.

The other road is the antithesis of the first. Many sexual abuse victims will choose a rigid, Puritanical lifestyle, giving no prerogative to sex or any other type of inter-gender contact. The Puritan is mentally disciplined and is capable of denial so strong that the sexual urge is eventually eliminated. This response is predominately found within those victims who have sought healing in the church only to be disappointed. Though it appears to be more spiritual that the first form, its effect upon a marriage is equally devastating.

WHORE AND LUST SPIRITS

In women, the lowest level of demonization in the sexual arena is a whore spirit. This is the typical level of demonization and will therefore confine itself to the inward focus. A whore spirit will rule the woman by the guilt associated with promiscuity. She will appear to be very loose morally, while holding to strict standards of morality in most other areas of her life. She will not just appear to love sex, but she will be consumed by it. The demon, in this internal, inward focus, will drive her to find approval and security in performing sexual acts. This level of demonization may include anyone who is characterized as the "easy girl" on through those characterized as nymphomaniacs. Though marriage is often attempted, she will find it nearly impossible to remain married. She may move from relationship to relationship trying to find love and security. She might also be extremely lonely, easily alienating and intimidating other women, while feeling much more comfortable in the company of men.

The male version of the whore spirit will likely be diagnosed as a demon of lust. Pornography will be the main focus of his life, in that, he will never be able to find enough perfect women to feed his obsession. He will not be able to get sex off his mind for more than a few minutes at a stretch, so he will entertain continual sexual daydreams. In the church, he may appear to be prudish about sexual issues and will not engage in sexual innuendo or banter, fearing discovery of his secret sin. All the while this man will be trapped in his loneliness, craving intimacy, but finding only a flawed counterfeit.

While there are many of these men in the church, few are ever unmasked. They have come to the church trying to find help for their issue, but help for real sexual issues is rare. The subject is not one commonly discussed within the cultured and refined society of church. It is one of the great failures of the institutionalized church. While prim and proper sermons are being delivered weekly, the men in the pew are in bondage to pornography and are under siege by demons of lust. The issue is left in the closet and finds approval in the embarrassed silence of the church leadership. The only reason for such silence is that the level of perversion in the pew only mirrors the level of perversion in the pulpit. Over the past decade, we have ministered to pastors from a variety of denominations trapped in the grasp of lust. They are guilt-ridden and powerless to stop it. Most have graduated from secretly buying porn magazines to using the ever-present internet to sustain their addiction. Each year more revelations are made of supposed men of God falling into sexual sin. They have affairs with their secretaries, the organist or the choir director. The many men who are caught in this sin are just the tip of the iceberg lurking under the surface.

This attack is unprecedented upon the earth. The evil forces are free to step up their offensive upon the leadership of the Western church since the culture is so completely devoid of morals. The tendency is to judge oneself in relation to the culture rather than by the standards of Scripture. One client shared how his pastor makes it a habit to instruct men within his congregation who struggle with sexual sin that it is permissible to look at pornography. What is important, according to this double-minded shepherd, is what you are doing while you are looking at pictures of naked women. His justification is this: when one is not masturbating while looking at pornography he is not sinning. His testimony includes his liberation from addiction to pornography. However, I was once asked by his daughter to fix something on their home computer. While checking it out, I clicked on his internet history menu. Down came a whole list of sites that had been recently visited, including Playboy.com.

Since he is participating in it himself, he cannot find a way to urge those men in his congregation caught in the same snare to find freedom. He is one example of many pastors whose lives are being destroyed by pornography. Is it any wonder those in the pews cannot be free?

THE OUTWARD FOCUS

The host of a Sex-based control spirit is suffering under the same destructive influences as those above while radiating the external portion of the unclean spirit's work. The outward influence of this type of control spirit is the easiest to explain. Every man in the room will know when a woman carrying this type of spirit enters the room, whether or not he is looking in her direction. Heads will turn; eyes will shift.

She's here, and every man knows it.

At this juncture, women always think I exaggerate. I do no such thing. When my three girls were growing up, I kept telling them about the male of the species. My favorite saying was, "Guys thinks with their zippers." Though they heard me say this a thousand times, they were still confused by the reactions of boys when they were dating. Women readers, please just take my word on this. Men are brute beasts when it comes to the female of the species and when demonic influence is added, the vulnerability of the gender is even more evident.

We met Pete and Polly at a hotel. They flew across the country to undergo deliverance. I was introduced to Pete and then he turned to introduce me to his wife, Polly. As I reached across the table to shake her hand, I let out an inadvertent gasp and withdrew my hand before shaking hers. Luckily, I had just washed my hands and I quickly explained that they were still wet. My spiritual eyes were open in preparation for the deliverance session, and when I leaned across the table to shake Polly's hand, her Sex-based control spirit leapt up and took me by surprise.

I withdrew my hand so the spirit could not transfer to me in any way. This is the operation of a familiar spirit. It may transfer from a demonized person by physical contact, through entering into covenant with someone, or when the unsuspecting person has a breach in his/her spiritual security. A breach might be through weakness in the same area as the unclean spirit's function. Now, I was not living out some secret sexual sin, but I know that I am a man, and, as such, am weak in this area. When I withdrew from Polly, I immediately moved close to my wife for protection. You might even say that I hid behind her skirts. Listen, when one thinks one is invulnerable to attack, attack will surely come and one can be easily overcome. I am no hero. Working in deliverance for a couple of decades has proved this very clearly.

I refused to come anywhere near Polly until her deliverance was over.

The session commenced in their hotel room. We had six team members, with Pete and Polly sitting together in the middle. We dealt with Pete first. Then, it was Polly's turn. Though I was seeing the Sex-based control spirit very clearly, I waited as each of the team members shared what he/she was seeing or sensing. They were all completely blinded. The other two men on the team were former pastors and have served with us many times. They were two babbling idiots in this session. I was a little frustrated with what they were telling me about the spirits they discerned. I had forgotten that each of them had been delivered of one level of lust or another and that they remained extremely sensitive to the effects thereof. Their contribution was completely ridiculous. One pastor's wife was sitting on the bed within just a couple feet of Polly. Since a spirit of lust had ruled her husband before his deliverance, she was overly sensitive to the effects of this spirit and she was not helpful either. The other pastor's wife rambled on about seeing Polly as a little girl sitting in a little red wagon. She gave no interpretation of the little vision, so I was left alone to diagnose Polly.

I am committed to acquiring the voice of two or three witnesses in a spiritual matter such as deliverance, so I was in a quandary. Since my wife had conducted pre-deliverance counseling with Polly, I could not ask her what she saw. I asked the Holy Spirit what to do and I felt like He indicated that Pete could participate as Polly's spiritual covering without violating the criteria of spiritual, rather than natural knowledge.

I said, "Pete, if there were an unclean spirit harassing your wife, what do you think it would be?" His response was immediate, "Well, there's a perverse thing going on there!" I said, "That's close enough. I'll take it."

After the session, Polly was confused by our diagnosis. We spent a couple of hours trying to explain it to her, until a light bulb went on. She told us about having a flat tire on the highway. She asked, "Could that be why within about ten minutes, there was a whole crowd of men stopped to help me?"

Duh.

The Control

The motivation of the inward focus of this sort of demonization is to provide safety, to preempt abuse, and to endeavor to fill the great void of worthlessness in the self-image of the host. The external focus may be dual in nature. Much of what is being done for and to the target of such control is to use sex to endear the target to the host. Misuse of sex damages the self-image of the host and the target is used as fodder to satisfy the craving for worthiness. The essential need of a person hosting any type of control spirit is to obligate the target to the host, thereby obligating the target to do whatever the host requires. With the host of a Sex-based control spirit, this need is frequently as simple as craving worth. Though simple to understand, the need to be worth something in the eyes of someone is an essential and valid need.

The presence of the unclean spirit only compounds the

craving until it becomes the ruling focus of one's life. Therefore, the life of one captive to a Sex-based control spirit is cyclic in nature and the product is devastation. The person will have been sexually abused at a young age, hence the initial devastation. The devastation demands healing. The primitive mind of the child leaps to the obvious solution: the abuser wants sex; if I give it, perhaps he/she will not hurt me anymore and/or he/she will like me if I give him/her what he/she wants. The sex act brings more devastation and reinforces the devastation with disappointment. The only solution is to give more of them more of what they want.

Thus the cycle of abuse continues.

Within the cycle lies a wildcard providing more confusion for the victim. Because Father created humans with the sex drive for our enjoyment, the victim of sexual abuse will experience enjoyment within the abusive, destructive pattern. When he/she enjoys it, he/she then experiences a greater level of guilt than is normally associated with such activity. Thus, the confusion surrounding the experience is exacerbated. It becomes so powerful that the victim is unable to discern the difference between what is harmful and what is helpful.

THE PATH TO WHOLENESS

The focus of the wholeness process after deliverance includes much of what has already been shared for those recovering from other control spirit influences. However, recovery for the host of a Sex-based control spirit must include some additional elements. These will include redeveloping the self-image of the victim and the beliefs about sex or sexual identity. We have found an interesting phenomenon among these recoverees. One of two things occurs regarding mirrors. One group is unable to look at themselves in a mirror. Many have never seen themselves naked, most dress without the use of a mirror, and their husbands rarely catch a glimpse of their naked wives. The level of shame is overwhelming and their nakedness only reinforces their sense of vulnerability.

The other group is obsessed with themselves in the mirror and otherwise. They obsess about clothes, jewelry, and makeup. They are seldom seen outside of the perfect image they have contrived for themselves. The only thing that makes them feel comfortable and safe is the near-perfect image of their sexually desirable persona. They thrive on attention, and they attract the opposite gender like flies and repel their own gender. Conversation will never go beyond the superficial, because it will reveal that there is nothing beneath the perfect image they so fiercely protect. Sexual innuendo will be salted freely into their banter, producing laughter from men and disapproval from women.

For each group, recovery is remarkably simple. For the Puritans, their level of sexual awareness must be raised. For the self-absorbed group, they must be taught to turn it down and focus their attention on other areas of life. For some bound in Puritanism, our counselors have encouraged them to take stock of their physical features by looking at themselves in a full-length mirror in the privacy of their own homes declaring Scriptures such as *"I praise you because I am fearfully and wonderfully made"* (Psalm 139:14). This simple step may take many weeks to accomplish for the first time, but seems to be a watershed moment in their recovery. For the second group, we urge them to stop wearing makeup, to wear modest clothing and to avoid their jewelry box for a time to break the hold these things have on their self-image. Of course, these are only two extreme examples of what might be expected of them, but it should reveal the degree to which they may have to go to break these powerful forces in their lives.

Lightning In A Bottle

Admittedly, recovery from a Sex-based control spirit is a

little like trying to put lightning back into a bottle after it has been released. Sex has a force all its own, powered by the creative hand of the Most High. However, regulating it is the very definition of Christian responsibility. Though we have been given liberty and freedom in all things, restraint is the evidence of spiritual growth. The Word encourages us to be *"temperate in all things"* (I Corinthians 9:25 KJV). This is drawn from the picture of the athlete in training for the competition. To gain the prize, he must restrain himself from indulging in any sort of excess, whether food, leisure, or sexual activity.

Therefore, wholeness is achieved for the Puritan group through finding an appropriate expression of their sexuality within the context of marriage. One recoveree was heard to ask her counselor, "Does this mean we have to *like* sex?" The answer frightened and challenged her: "Yes." Since then, her husband has expressed exuberant joy at his wife's pursuit of intimacy with him.

For the second group, confining themselves to one spouse and finding a depth of intimacy is the goal. Either way, sex must gravitate from a biological act to the intimate expression of worth. In this, one will find wholeness.

Chapter 12

THE SPIRIT OF JEZEBEL

SEARCHING FOR JEZEBEL

For purposes of identification, we have found that the most powerful manifestation of the female control spirit is the spirit of Jezebel. We will take a look at the Biblical Jezebel in a later chapter, but for now we should make a few things clear. Having dealt with hundreds of these spirits over the nine years since Katie's deliverance, we can make some confident statements about them.

We have never found the spirit of Jezebel inhabiting a man. They are always found in women. A Jezebelian spirit can be the ruling Principality or Power over a church, a city, or a region—all of which contain men—but at the level of individual demonization, control spirits in men fall into a category of their own which we have identified as Luciferian spirits or the spirit of Lucifer.

Jezebel has been used by leadership in some portions of the Church to target strong women who have the audacity to disagree or to express their opinion. What well-meaning Christian lady would dare fight the accusation that she is a Jezebel if it came from leadership? If she is a committed believer, she might accept the rebuke while not entirely understanding the accusation. More often, the abused lady will fight back, the inevitable results of which are church splits, more brokenness, and destroyed people.

It is our counsel that one must never accuse someone of being under the influence of an unclean spirit, no matter what the spirit is. This wisdom goes double for calling someone Jezebel. When those holding levels of spiritual authority use the indictment, the victim of such spiritual abuse may be permanently damaged. Therefore, here is wisdom: never call someone a Jezebel. Never. Remember, those under the influence of any type of control spirit are rarely aware of the unclean spirit's presence. When making such an accusation, all it accomplishes is to reinforce the demon's hold. A woman under Jezebel's manipulation will be so deeply entrenched that the unclean spirit will be an integral part of the woman's personality, paradigms, and relationships. If she is unaware there is a demon present, all one accomplishes by making this accusation is to abuse her further.

A friend of mine, we'll call him Carl, experienced the wrath of Jezebel firsthand. Carl travels as an itinerate prophet. One Sunday morning before the service began, he approached the pastor, saying he had received a specific word for the church. Carl asked the pastor whether he wanted the fresh prophetic word or the sermon he had come prepared to deliver. The pastor immediately chose the prophetic word. Carl obediently delivered the word to the congregation, the crux of which was the command to "be nice to one another."

At the pastor's home that evening, Carl was confronted by the pastor's wife. She expressed her concern with what he had shared in his Sunday morning sermon. The conversation took a bit of a turn and, in his exuberance to speak the truth, Carl told the pastor that his wife was Jezebel. By the time the smoke cleared, Carl's reputation was completely destroyed and his sermon topic had been reinterpreted to be the rantings of a woman-hating madman. The pastor and his wife made it their mission to make sure no one invited Carl back to preach in their area or in any place across the country where they had contacts. Carl is now very careful with his tongue.

If it is still unclear, here it is in plain English: stop it, shut up, hold your tongue, and never speak the accusation in her presence.

The Nature of Jezebel

A Jezebelian spirit is a hybrid of all the types of control spirits active in women. This spirit will employ all of the other tactics of control spirits as described in the previous chapters. They will be employed singularly and in combination with one another, tailored to control the circumstance in the most effective manner possible making it impossible to pin her symptoms down. She will at one moment be a meek lamb for whom one should feel sorry, and the next moment she will be in a frenetic rage driving those involved through the paces of her manipulation. All of these mechanisms are available for her and she will move from one to the next with lightning speed, all of which makes life miserable for those with whom she has relationship.

However, there is an additional component that sets her apart from the other control spirits and makes her inherently dangerous in the Church. This final piece of the puzzle is the religious nature of Jezebel. Her motivation and focus is religious control. She may appear to the innocent observer to be the most spiritual of the bunch. She is usually powerfully prophetic. She will be ready to serve in any weak area of the church's program that will cultivate her grasp on the leadership. Finally, when she has taken control of the pastor, the leadership and the church as a whole, it will be too late to do anything about it. She will work to maintain her image of spirituality while ruling the entire church with veiled power.

Access to this sort of control by Jezebel is often achieved through intercession groups. Jezebelian spirits gravitate to intercession ministries for several reasons. First, an intercessor has the ear of the leadership. Any problems, issues, concerns, or vision will be presented to the intercessory team for prayer. This becomes a powerful position. She will use it to speak into the lives and ministries of those in authority to further her own agenda. Then, as she gains the blessing of the leadership, she can wield control over as many other people as possible through the intercessor's group. She will manipulate prophetic word to ensure that she receives the credit and a pat on the back from leadership. She will use her status to create power plays in order to grow in power and authority in the fellowship. In the end, she may use her position to overthrow the pastor or other leadership in order to install herself into control.

In any case, it remains vital to our understanding to know that this is the work of an unclean spirit functioning through an unsuspecting woman. Often, she possesses no knowledge of the underlying agenda of the unclean spirit. If confronted with such information, she will adamantly defend her pure motives. In sharing this information with pastors and leadership teams, we have often found them unable or unwilling to separate the outward action of the demon from the person. Subsequently, the battle develops between flesh and blood rather than between leadership and the spirit realm. In the end, each party is defeated by the clever schemes of the unclean spirit.

The following is a typical scenario. The host of the Jezebelian spirit will begin attending a church. She appears to be a capable, intelligent woman, just the person the leadership has been looking for to oversee one area of ministry or another. Soon, the host will ingratiate herself to the pastor, the leadership team, and the people by serving selflessly, fervently, and capably. Her gifts will fit into the vision and philosophy of the Body and all will be well in this little slice of heaven.

Her current position, however, will not be enough for the demon. The unclean spirit will drive her to greater heights of authority and power until she begins to openly question the leadership. "One of the primary ways in which Jezebel makes inroads into a church is through seduction—whether emotionally, spiritually, or sexually."[18] Using any or all of these tactics, she will be capable of swaying the votes and the hearts of the church people until they are unable to see anything but her way of thinking. In the end, she will lead the charge to oust the pastor in favor of someone--though she would never say so—who can be controlled. This scenario, with minor variations, has been carried out hundreds of times. The church is left under the control of the Jezebelian spirit and no one is the wiser.

The host of a Jezebelian spirit will often appear to be completely submitted to her husband and to the leadership of the church. She will be trained by the unclean spirit to manipulate subtly rather than with obvious tactics. Although, when she is backed into a corner, she will be capable of striking out with such force that the recipient of such an attack will be left decimated and demoralized. This is the place in which many pastors find themselves. Their only course of action is to either capitulate to the demands of the woman or to step into the ring with her and go to war. A war of this magnitude will often turn out in the favor of the Jezebelian spirit. The reason is the pastor or leadership team will generally attack the problem in the natural, that is, by discussion, logic, or discipline, when the issue is entirely spiritual in nature. Unless the victims of the attack are experienced in spiritual warfare, the fight is lost before it begins.

INHERENT AUTHORITY

According to Scripture, the male of the species has been given an inherent authority that has been withheld from the female. We see the first glimpse of it in the curse he spoke over Eve. *"To the woman he said, 'I will greatly increase your pains in childbearing; with pain you will give birth to children. Your desire will be for your husband, and he will rule over you'"* (Genesis 3:16). Some have taught that the effects of this curse have been removed at the Cross, saying the woman is completely and in every way equal to man. In the case of salvation, giftedness, and anointing, we find this to be accurate.

The pursuit of sound doctrine requires us to examine whether or not the work of the Cross completely eliminated the effects of the curse Father spoke on that day. First, behold the serpent. Once Jesus' labor on the Cross was completed, did snakes regain the legs they obviously possessed prior to the curse? Certainly not. What about Adam? If you have ever done any gardening, you will know that Adams's curse is still in effect. The ground is cursed to this day, several thousand years later, effortlessly producing thorns, thistles and weeds, while the seeds purposefully planted come up only through sweat and toil. In addition, man's body still returns to dust upon death, just as the Lord commanded. So, for the serpent and for the man, the curse remains intact, despite the complete work of the Cross.

Finally, we must review the curse upon the woman. Apparently, prior to the fall into sin, the woman was intended to bear children with a minimum or the absence of pain. It seems absurd to even address the question of how horribly painful childbirth is to the mother. After seeing my oldest daughter sweating and crying (among other things) to produce my first granddaughter, I can assure any of you skeptics out there that this part of the curse is in full operation.

But, what about the rest of the curse? *"Your desire will be for your husband, and he will rule over you."* On the face of it, there seem to be two diverse thoughts crammed together in this one sentence. We are convinced that there are not two, but one thought. *"Your desire will be for your husband"* cannot be separated from *"and he will rule over you."* Certainly, the latter portion makes it clear the man has been given inherent authority to "rule" over the woman, but what about this *desire*? It is possible this *desire* is just emotional in nature, that is, to *need* him. However, it seems to demand more. We offer the opinion that within this curse there was implanted a competitive spirit to covet his position of authority.

It is inconceivable that to "desire" one's husband could be considered a *curse* in any other arena except in this competition for authority. If it truly were a curse, its fruit would not be a strong marriage bond, which such an emotional *desire* would indicate. Instead, it must be equal to the definition of a curse as defined by the curses upon the serpent and the man.

The curse indicates the competitive nature of the male-female relationship. The woman is naturally predisposed to compete for the rulership in relationship with the man. Replacing the word "and" with the word "but" could help us to better understand the implication of the curse. *"Your desire will be for your husband but he will rule over you"* This is used only for clarification not to change Scripture. At the point of conception, the female is endowed with female organs, female paradigms, female hormones, the ability to produce children, and the craving to rule over the man. This natural craving is fertile ground for inhabitation of the spirit of Jezebel. Adding to it abuse, hurt, and destruction at the hands of stronger males, the female heart essentially bursts forth as fallow ground for demonic habitation.

In the end, if the curses upon the serpent survive the intervention of the work of the Cross, as well as the curses upon the man, and the curse of pain on childbirth remains, it only stands to reason the curse is still valid giving the man inherent authority over the woman. The only question, then, is what does the man do with such authority? Does he use it as a license to abuse and demean the woman? Or does he do what is implicit in Paul's writings concerning headship?

This is the beginning of wisdom on this subject. *"Now I want you to realize that the head of every man is Christ, and the head of the woman is man, and the head of Christ is God"* (I Corinthians 11:3). The relationship between Christ and God ('Christ' indicating the time while in His earthly ministry) is not a doormat relationship. On the contrary, the relationship elevated and exalted Christ to a place of great honor, i.e. sitting at the right hand of the Father (Hebrews 12:2). What about the relationship between Christ and man? This relationship, too, exalted man from lowly human dust to become the very child of God (I John 3:1-2) and the right to actually become exactly like Him when we see Him. How marvelous and remarkable is this fact!

So here comes the final relationship listed in this verse. If the relationship between God and Christ and between Christ and man exalts the lower, so, too, must the relationship between man and the woman exalt, lift up, and elevate her, until she feels as thrilled to be the "lesser" as the man is thrilled with being the "lesser" in Christ, and Christ is thrilled to be the "lesser" before Father. If men could grasp this revelation they would not need to demand: "Obey me, after all, the Bible says I am the head of the home."

Chapter 13

JEZEBEL IN ACTION

JEZEBEL HATES AUTHORITY

Jezebel is a spirit who inhabits the female of the species. The unclean spirit inhabits the natural state of the woman, in addition to the destruction of whatever abuse she has suffered, and inflates her natural tendency to desire to rule into a full-blown war against authority. She will oppose any authority other than her own. She will intimidate and overpower any other woman who attempts to gain power over her. She may be able to suffer under another's rule for a time, but it will not be long before she steps into the position of power toward which the unclean spirit drives her.

However, as much as she hates female authority, male authority cannot be tolerated. This intolerance can best be seen in the rabid nature of feminists in modern culture. It has been reported that most, if not all, of the leading feminists in the country are childhood victims of sexual abuse. Many of their fathers abandoned them, as well. Their natural response to such tragic circumstances is to hate all men as surrogates for those who hurt them so deeply. This trauma is enough to fuel the movement to overthrow all male authority. When inhabited by the spirit of Jezebel, this fuel is ignited into an unquenchable inferno devouring both the woman and the man she abhors.

Within the Church, the struggle takes on supernatural proportions.

The Inner Struggle

Christian women who desire to grow and draw near to Father desire to find the reality of the safety and protection of the man's headship covering. Many of our clients tell about the conflict within them as they endeavor to submit to their husbands as unto the Lord (Ephesians 5:22-24) while being driven to degrade and diminish their husbandly authority. It is one thing to submit "to the Lord" as the perfect Son of God, but entirely another to submit to an imperfect, sometimes brain-dead human husband.

Without an understanding of deliverance, she remains conflicted. The unclean spirit has the legal right to inhabit the dark, unbelieving part of her heart. He does so fiercely. Still, she has given her life to Christ and her longing is to serve Him completely. However, her husband is there, standing in his God-given spiritual authority, acting for the entire world like a "stupid, stupid man."

What's a girl to do?

A married woman hosting a Jezebelian spirit will, almost without exception, be convinced that her husband is the one with control issues. This will spring out of her corrupted perception of male authority. She will inwardly burn because he will not stand up and take his spiritual position in the home. At the same moment, she will demean him in an attempt to keep him in his place.

We have listened to hundreds of complaints from women who are angry at their husband's inability to take their rightful place of authority. The voice of the Holy Spirit is urging them to submit, while the unclean spirit's voice demands that the men be crushed for their weakness. The result is an incessant inner struggle with little hope of resolution.

JEZEBEL EMASCULATES MEN

Because Jezebelian spirits hate authority and because the male of the species has inherent authority, the goal of these spirits is to emasculate men. This concept is also true in the lower levels of the Jezebelian agenda. The husbands of women with control spirits can easily be broad-brushed into one stereotypical model. They are often what might be termed "soft men." I do not mean to say that they are necessarily effeminate, but they are usually good-natured, sensitive men. Even if they are what might be said to be very manly—hunters, fishermen, Nascar fans—they usually have a softer side regarding women.

Hidden under this nice, sensitive façade can be found a man stripped, or in the process of being, stripped of his manly authority. The words, "Yes, dear" are never far from his lips. He may be a leader elsewhere, but with a little detective work one will find that his wife wears the pants in his family. She cannot allow her husband to be in authority over her because of the damage done by the trauma and the influence of the ruling spirit in her life.

In many cases, the host of a Jezebelian spirit will hold a job that pays more than her husband makes. This is a source of great pride for the unclean spirit and for the host. It proves she is better than the man and gives her the right to rule the money earned by the household.

One pastor's wife, we will call her Carla, carrying a very powerful Jezebelian spirit, confided in a friend how much she earned in her vocation. Her pastor husband served in a small church that paid him very little. She remarked, "I earn the real money and my husband does ministry for a hobby." Because this is true, she demands equal time in the pulpit while her husband stands nearby with a compliant, obedient look on his face.

When faced with the necessity of deliverance, Carla devised a brilliant plan to dupe the pre-deliverance counselor into believing that her husband was a controller who was verbally abusive, mean, and demanding. I was that counselor. Because they were pastors, it was necessary for me to lead the deliverance session. Because I relied upon the natural knowledge obtained in the pre-deliverance session, we attempted to cast a control spirit out of her husband and pretended to cast a spirit of rejection out of Carla.

We were completely taken in by the unclean spirit.

Since her deliverance session, Carla has been given new veracity in her brokenness. She is now running nearly every portion of the ministry and has moved into positions of authority in the intercessory groups in her region. I learned a tremendous lesson through Carla's non-deliverance. She, among other tragic mistakes in deliverance ministry, is the reason we teach the necessity of removing anyone who has natural knowledge of the client, whenever possible. Her husband remains weak and powerless, frustrated at his lack of spiritual authority in the church. He is unwilling to allow us to rectify our mistake since he has paid so high an emotional price for the first session.

THE CENTER OF ALL THINGS

The paradox here is that the host of a Jezebelian spirit will most likely appear to be the greatest servant you have ever seen. Church boards are filled with people who appear to be serving the good of the Body, while their true agenda is grasping for power and authority in order to build their own ego.

Hosts of Jezebelian spirits are all that and more.

All control spirits seek control for the safety and security of the host. This is what makes her tactics seem appropriate in her mind. It is seldom verbalized or even pondered. It just is. Therefore, anything threatening the control of the host immediately becomes the enemy. The unclean spirit serves as a vigilant watchman over everyone and everything with which the host comes into contact. So, everything is about the host.

Lilly held forty-two jobs in the church. She was the organist, the Sunday School Superintendent, the Women's ministry leader, the treasurer, the Director of Missions, and everything else possible. She was selfless and giving. She was there every time the church doors were open. In fact, she was the one who was there early to open them. She volunteered for every vacant position. She filled in when others were sick. She worked a fulltime job and aptly cared for her husband and children.

She appeared to be the perfect Proverbs Thirty-One woman.

As we developed relationship with Lilly, we found an angry, powerless wreck lurking beneath her perfect exterior. It was many years later that we discovered the real truth of Lilly's life. She was the daughter of missionaries. As a child, she was placed in a missionary kids home whenever her parents were on the field. In this purposed "safe," Christian environment, Lilly was repeatedly sexually abused by one of the house parents.

After years of abuse, she graduated and set about finding a husband. As is the case with many such women, Lilly's choice of a husband was a non-threatening, soft man. She hated him for his weakness, but her hatred was masked by the perfect Christian wife shtick she developed to mask her true feelings.

She worked hard for the Lord in every job she could find. She did so to impress Father, in hopes of obtaining His approval. In her pain, she never found His approval, so she worked harder, was more pious, gave more money to the church and eventually disintegrated from the inside out.

The Jezebelian spirit inhabiting the dark places of Lilly's heart drove her to the point of a nervous breakdown. She entertained thoughts of suicide. She hated herself and everyone around her, though she maintained the outward appearance of the perfect Christian woman.

When she finally underwent deliverance, the relief was apparent in her demeanor. She has learned to be free to serve Father in a few areas of ministry with joy. She fell in love with her husband all over again. Lilly is now a well-adjusted, joyful member of the Body of Christ instead of the driven, joyless religious person trying to gain the approval of the Heavenly Father.

Religious, More Religious, Most Religious

We have witnessed a strange phenomenon in most victims of Jezebelian spirits. The work of the demon is to provide what is lacking in the person in order that she might not need to seek out help from the Living God. However, when the host of the control spirit seeks out such help and becomes born again, the character of the demon's work changes. Now, instead of resisting religion in the life of the host, the demon's tactics invert and they press the person into religious performance to the point of legalism. Many born again hosts of Jezebelian spirits become rigid, rabid Christians. Because they are subject to the fear of being out-of-control, the demonic influence manipulates them into a performance-based, rule-oriented Christianity.

This excess appears to provide the needed spiritual safety within a religious system and leaves no room for insecurities in their relationship with Father. In fact, relationships are often difficult and most times impossible for the host of a Jezebelian spirit. Not only is her relationship with Father characterized by rules and bondage, but also her relationships with others reflect the same obsession with control. Control is the ruin of any relationship. However, the host of a control spirit will be controlling with her spouse, her children and her friends. In the immortal words of a controller, "What I do is for their own good."

This religious nature has been demonstrated throughout history as the principality Jezebel manifested herself through Diana of the Ephesians (Acts 19:23-34 KJV) and other Queen of Heaven cults.[19] In the end, she will be revealed as the Great

Harlot of Revelation 17. She is strictly religious and bound in pietism. Still, as all the rules and laws remain unsatisfying, the victim is continually victimized by whatever religious system she has chosen.

Chapter 14

AHAB AND JEZEBEL

INTRODUCING THE HISTORICAL JEZEBEL

Ahab was the king. Jezebel was his queen. Only, she didn't quite see it that way. Jezebel was not at all impressed with the kingship of her husband, other than to further her own agenda in the country of Israel. "Jezebel was the evil genius behind Ahab, without whom she was a serpent without fangs."[20] She was royalty herself, being the daughter of a ruthless king who was also a priest of Ashera (or Astarte).[21] Her name and background defined her then, and define the spirit who emulates her today.

Our introduction to Jezebel comes in I Kings 16 when Ahab, king of Israel, took her as his wife contrary to the explicit command of the Lord against marriage to any of the peoples of Canaan (Deuteronomy 7:3). The name Jezebel means "where is Baal; a seeker of Baal."[22] Her father was Ethbaal, meaning "living with Baal or enjoying the favor of Baal"[23], who murdered his predecessor to ascend to the throne of Sidon. Tyre and Sidon were two cities located very close together, notable only that the principle temple of Baal was located in Tyre. "Baal was the principle male deity of the Phoenicians and Canaanites, ... and as the sun-god, was worshipped as the supporter and first principle of psychical life and of the generative and reproductive power of nature."[24] Ahab's heart was set on doing evil in the sight of God, so Jezebel made the perfect helper for him. She helped him move the entire country of Israel into Baal worship.

THE TEMPLE OF BAAL

One of the first influences of Jezebel we see upon Ahab was the building of a temple for Baal similar to the one in Tyre (I Kings 16:32). This construction project was in direct violation of the law of God and solidified Baal worship within the Hebrew culture. To worship Baal was to replace the true God with a substitute. There could be no greater blasphemy. Throughout the reign of Jezebel and Ahab, the worship of Baal remained the primary focus of the kingdom. They went so far as to oppose the prophet of God, Elijah, in a showdown of spiritual authority and power on Mount Carmel.

This action revealed the corrupt nature and character of Ahab. He had set his heart to follow after the Baals and his queen provided the impetus for such wickedness. He was quick to follow the evil nature of his ancestors and was powerless to break free from its captivity.

OTIS AND JASMINE

When a woman inhabited by a Jezebelian spirit marries, she will seldom choose a man of strong character. Rather, her choice will be someone who harbors insecurities, fears, and may reflect a propensity to be ruled by a woman. He will already be subject to a spirit of Ahab or, as is often the case, he will simply be fertile ground for its introduction. Should the host of a Jezebelian spirit marry a strong, charismatic man, one of two things is sure to occur. They may coexist for a time, but the unclean spirit will demand control, cause a death struggle, followed by the ultimate goal: divorce. The only other course of action is for Jezebel to create her Ahab. Some are born Ahabs, while other Ahabs are made. This process is excruciating.

Otis was the top salesman in his company. Over the years he had sold everything imaginable door to door. In his latest company, his fellow salesmen revered him and he won every promotion offered. He feared no one. He was self confident and charismatic. Then he met Jezebel. Jezebel, let's call her Jasmine, was beautiful and willing to cheat on her husband with Otis. Eventually, Jasmine left her husband and married Otis.

At that time, Otis' salary was well into six figures. Jasmine loved his strength and authority for a while. But soon, her subservient role began to aggravate her. The demon within her devised a plan. As she flattered Otis for his exalted position within the company, she subtly laid the foundation for him to leave and start his own company competing with his former employer. She convinced Otis that she should be the president of the new company. He agreed.

The business was a smash. They opened numerous offices across the state and in the money rolled. All was well until the Jezebelian spirit began to tighten the noose around Otis' neck. Within just a few years the business went under and the failure destroyed Otis. After that, the unclean spirit demeaned and degraded Otis constantly and dismantled him piece by piece. Jasmine happily assumed the role of breadwinner for the household, while Otis became unable to sell anything to anyone, a powerless Ahab. Otis is now a weak, frail, sickly old man. The work of the demon is complete. The male authority has been destroyed and the Jezebelian spirit is now in control.

THE AHAB SPIRIT

There is seldom, if ever, a Jezebel without an Ahab. There must be a man who is made subservient to the Jezebelian spirit so that the purpose of the spirit's presence is fulfilled. It is important to remember that Ahab is a king by birth. His authority is inherent on two levels both as a male and as a king.

An Ahab within the Body of Christ may demonstrate his kingly authority on occasion, unless his wife is also involved in his ministry. He will be capable, intelligent, and useful to the Body. He will appear to be the greatest guy in the world. He will carry a powerful anointing. He will be easy to talk to and will most likely be coveted by other women in the fellowship. This may not manifest itself sexually, but the simple fact that he is not threatening to them endears him to women. He is utterly conflicted torn between impotency and kingship.

Ahab often comes off schizophrenic. Because he is under Jezebel's power, he is alternatively explosive then apologetic, or whiny then angry, etc. He is deeply confused because he torn in different directions. He eagerly wants to please, but he can't decide who to please first. He *rarely* makes the right choice: To please YHWH first. He is frustrated, longing for someone to simply *put him out of his misery and tell him what to do*. Jezebel is only too happy to oblige.[25]

We have discovered that some of the most dynamic preachers and consummate pastors suffer under the weight of an Ahab spirit. The kingly portion of their character will slip through in spite of the cruel dominion of Jezebel. However, in the home, they become the subservient, hen-pecked husband. "Husbands who submit to a wife with a Jezebel spirit beware, for she is like a black widow spider: She will kill and slowly suck the life out of her mate."[26] Whether he is in ministry or in business, Ahab is a king everywhere but in his own home.

Since Jezebel is consumed with ruling, her union with Ahab provides the ideal platform needed to exercise control. The nature of Jezebel is expressed through the religious, so many women carrying such spirits will seek out and marry men entering the pastorate. Within the corporate structure of the church, Jezebel operates freely, controlling both male and female sheep. She will use Ahab's authority to move into positions of authority, fiercely wielding her control.

Some Ahabs are so shell-shocked from the constant battles with their Jezebels that they will not be able to function in their gifts, anointing, or even talents. The Ahab spirit, in conjunction with the spirit of Jezebel will constrict their level of authority to such an extent that they may sit in her shadow content to follow her around like a puppy dog.

This pattern is ubiquitous within Western culture. Nearly every sitcom on television illustrates the same combination. The wife is strong, confident, intelligent, and in charge. The husband is a likeable, bumbling idiot. Jezebel is at work in our culture at such a level that this model has become the norm for society. Gone are the days of "Father Knows Best." It has been replaced by "Everyone Loves Raymond," where the husband is assailed by both his control spirit mother and his control spirit wife.

Ahab now reigns as the king of comedy.

Ahab As King

The first time we shared our discoveries concerning control spirits was in an inner city church. We were at a church conducting a conference on spiritual warfare. As I laid out the different types of control spirits and how they operated, the pastor sat on the edge of his seat, his eyes riveted to my face. Each time I walked by him, he spun in his seat in order to maintain eye contact. Throughout the entire teaching, I grew more and more uncomfortable with his staring. I thought he was furious with me.

When the service was over, the pastor disappeared. We usually went out to get something to eat following the service, but this day he was nowhere to be found. I was sure he was planning to cancel the rest of our meetings.

The next day before the service he came through the door and grabbed my arm. He said, "I have to talk to you." I knew this was it; we were done. However, as we stepped aside he began to tell me that the teaching was exactly what he needed to hear.

He had disappeared the previous day in order to fire some of his staff that he knew were under the influence of control spirits. In addition, he had laid down the law in his home with his control spirit wife and his control spirit mother. Then, he informed me that he was under the influence of the spirit of Ahab and he needed deliverance as soon as possible.

This pastor had traveled extensively preaching at large churches around the country. He shared with me the difference between the spiritual authority and anointing he was able to exercise on the road as opposed to how powerless and minimized he felt at home and at his church. The message about Jezebel had crystallized his thinking and he immediately set about putting his spiritual house in order. Even though I had not shared anything of the teaching on Ahab, the Holy Spirit had revealed it to him. Once his deliverance was complete, he moved into a higher level of spiritual authority in his ministry.

The lesson in this pastor's story is the revelation of the kingly nature of someone inhabited by the Ahab spirit. Almost every man harassed by this type of spirit marries someone hosting a Jezebelian spirit. Inevitably, these two seem to find each other and eventually produce destruction, not just in each other, but also in their children and everyone they touch.

Should one or the other undergo deliverance and subsequently pursue wholeness, the result may be disastrous. If Ahab is cast out and Jezebel remains, there are only two options, either deliverance for Jezebel or divorce. Once Ahab is cast out, the man will immediately begin to grow in his ability to exercise his authority, both as a man and as the king of his ministry. Because Jezebel is the ruling spirit in the relationship it is unwise to cast Ahab out first. We recommend waiting until the host of the Jezebelian spirit is ready for deliverance and then taking them both through together.

Conversely, when Jezebel is cast out first, we have discovered something remarkable. When the wife is pursuing wholeness in spite of her husband's reticence to undergo deliverance, with proper guidance, the outcome may be very different. Often, the man hosting an Ahab spirit may find the courage to choose deliverance on his own terms when the driving spirit of Jezebel is removed and the threat of overthrow disappears. The empirical evidence provided by his wife's wholeness is the key to his finding freedom.

A LITTLE AHAB

Though the other five types of control spirits are not of the diabolical nature of Jezebel, we find that there is still a strong tendency for each to find and marry a man with Ahab tendencies. Though she might not be a full-blown Jezebel, the female host of a control spirit still requires someone to dominate. The husband chosen may not carry a spirit of Ahab, but frequently he will possess many of the attributes we find in someone carrying a demon of Ahab.

We rarely find a married couple that both carry control spirits. The very nature of control spirits demands they remain in control. When both of the partners manifest control spirits, an explosion is likely. Should they make the mistake of marrying, the life expectancy of such a union is very short. A woman hosting a control spirit of any type will always endeavor to convince her husband that he is controlling. Therefore, she justifies her controlling behavior at his expense, making him the scapegoat. The likelihood that he is a controller is very slim. Typically, the husband will be sufficiently infected with Ahab that he will acknowledge his responsibility, weaken his authority enough to make her happy, so the marriage survives. When two people carrying control spirits do marry, it is likely that one will be aggressive and the other passive. For example, someone hosting a Fear-based or Martyr-based control spirit might marry someone with an Anger-based control spirit. But, again, this is very rare and the marriage will not prosper.

WHOLENESS FOR AHAB

For a host of an Ahab spirit to come to wholeness after deliverance only requires simple encouragement. The kingly anointing upon this man will quickly bloom once the constricting influences of the Ahab and the Jezebelian spirits are removed. We have joyfully released several hundred men from their grasp and have successfully guided them into powerful and compassionate ministries.

The one important caution that must be understood is the tendency for this newly freed man to spring from the ditch of subservience on one side of the road so forcefully that he is thrown across the proverbial road into the other ditch. This other ditch is the out-of-balance exercise of control. In essence, he may find the free use of authority so liberating it becomes a control issue for him. He may be disproportionately bossy, controlling or demanding until he can find the balance. This is the natural course of action in the wholeness process and should not be perceived as a permanent condition. Once he experiences the other ditch, he will be better equipped to avoid it in the future.

Most recovering Ahabs become useful and productive members of the Body of Christ. Their inherent authority as men and kings, when employed within the whole character of Christ, makes them invaluable to the Kingdom.

Chapter 15

THE LUCIFERIAN SPIRIT

MALE CONTROL SPIRITS

The pinnacle of demon-infested male control emerges in the form of a man under the influence of a Luciferian spirit. We have laid the foundation for the proper understanding of inherent male authority. When coupled with an unclean spirit mimicking the authority-grasping nature of Lucifer, the combination is horrific. The man hosting a Luciferian spirit is self-absorbed, power hungry, and authority seizing. He will likely be a workaholic. He will not be able to rest, since all authority is not yet his. His motivation will be so strong, vacations and even rest breaks will oppose his nature. He will be self-focused and goal-obsessed. He may be considered successful if his intelligence is comparable to his drive. If not, then he will work harder and longer hours, as if beating his head against a wall to break through and find accomplishment.

He will not be a happy camper.

He will likely neglect his family. Whatever time is given to his wife and children will be spent for the sole purpose of furthering his ambitions and stroking his ego. Publicly, he will appear to be very relational, even as his own family members are slipping through his fingers. He will be a strong disciplinarian as the children are growing up. His wife will cower under his cruel rule. She will likely suffer extremely low self-esteem. She will serve him with unwavering complicity to avoid coming under his whip. If she questions his rule, she will be punished severely. Usually, the punishment will be verbal abuse, intended to keep her in her place.

The first Luciferian spirit I recall encountering had been on his church's governing board for forty-two years when I became the pastor. Stanley's approach was simple and straightforward from the moment we met: anything brought to the table without his prior approval was summarily dismissed without so much as a discussion. His control of the church extended into every area. His most effective control tool was money. No one dared question him for fear of losing his substantial giving. He belittled women in particular and everyone in general. During one strained discussion regarding the direction of the church, Stanley turned to me across the conference table and said softly, "Pastors come and pastors go, but I am always here."

I took it as a challenge.

He was many decades my senior, so direct warfare was not an option. So, I went over his head to the Father. My prayer was this: "Lord, fix him or get him out." If I had engaged him in a natural battle, he could have destroyed everything the Lord wanted to accomplish there. The unclean spirit on him had destroyed a whole lineup of pastors before me. I understood my enemy; I went over his head. I honored him as my elder and never spoke against him or demeaned him in any way. I just prayed.

Within a couple of months, Stanley appeared at my office door demanding to speak with me. He marched in and tossed a sheet of paper onto my desk. I knew what it was before it landed. I read through the accusations and demeaning remarks searching for those two words for which I longed, and there they were: "I resign." He resigned from his position as head elder, board member, and, thankfully, his membership as well. He stood there waiting for me to talk him out of it. Instead, I took out a file folder, placed the resignation inside and put it into my desk drawer. I said gently, "Thank you, Mr. Turner." He stared at me in disbelief, his final control ploy having backfired.

WARRING AGAINST THE LUCIFERIAN SPIRIT

What came clear to me then and remains our strategy for spiritual warfare today is the power of the indirect attack. Men hosting Luciferian spirits (along with any other type of control spirit infestation) cannot be assaulted directly because they will be unaware of the presence of the ruling spirit. If they are confronted head-on, the result will certainly be further entrenchment into their dysfunctional behavior because they are forced into defending their position, even if they do not want to defend it. If someone near you is likely under the influence of such a spirit, go over his head. If you try to debate with him or convince him of his problem, he will undoubtedly trounce you soundly and then use his victory to augment his already powerful worldview.

Instead, take the war into the territory of the aggressor. It is about the unclean spirit the man is hosting, it is not a personality or character issue. It is a spiritual issue. Take the war to him in the spirit realm. Bless him with your mouth and with your heart, but take authority over the unclean spirit in its own realm. Pray, asking and believing. Make commands against the spirit's hold on him. Treat the man with respect. Be loving and affirming, all the while pounding the spirit's hold. Do not fight with him. Capitulate for the time being; it is a small price to pay for the possibility of seeing him set free. Even if it takes years, care for him while assaulting the spirit on every opportunity. When he suggests he needs help, do not give it to him. Often, the first volley is a control ploy. Respond as if you do not know what he means. This is not a lie; you must understand that your husband or brother or father or friend is not the enemy. The unclean spirit is your enemy and he is smarter than you. Be prepared to wait out the real encounter.

While being assaulted by a Luciferian spirit inhabiting Doug, an acquaintance of mine, I inadvertently employed the indirect attack. Doug was talking a mile a minute to the waiter, ordering everyone's food and essentially taking control of the entire meeting. It gave me a headache and made me a little angry. So, while keeping my eyes on Doug, I covered my mouth with my hand and began whispering in prayer using some other language. I was astonished when, in a matter of minutes, Doug was slouched in his chair complaining of a headache and saying, "You go ahead and order. I don't feel well." After that, every time Doug's unclean spirit took control, I prayed quietly and all was well. I should say that, finally, Doug recognized his demonization and was set free from the unclean spirit. When we get together now, I order my own food.

As the Holy Spirit of the Living God is given time to move, the man hosting a Luciferian spirit may press for help and healing just like Doug. We liken this to the Gerasene demoniac (Mark 5). The demons seemingly controlling the man had driven him to apparent destruction. They had almost total control. However, the man had enough authority over himself to come toward Jesus and fall down before Him. The demons spoke through him and begged not to be tortured. They knew who Jesus was immediately, yet they could not withstand the power of the man to come to Jesus. If the demons were so completely in control, why did they allow such a thing? They should have been able to drive the man in the opposite direction. Yet, they were unable to do so.

We identify this as a "coming to." Deliverance cannot be secured without the assent of the demonized person. As is demonstrated by this severe case of demonization, the person retains authority over himself, however minimal, even as he passively succumbs to the influence of the demon. To find deliverance, the demonized person must "come to" Father for help. It is an act of his will. A person talked into undergoing deliverance, participating just to please someone else, or doing it to get them off his back, will not find freedom. It must be an affirmative act of the will.

The most valuable component for successful deliverance from a Luciferian spirit is desperation. Unless the man is desperate for freedom, he will remain subject to the learned behavior acquired under the unclean spirit's influence and revert to his previous condition. Warfare prayer, then, should target that desperation. Until he is desperate, wait and pray. Frequently, we will not schedule the deliverance session for a couple of months so desperation is cultivated in his heart. Certainly, he may become angry at our delays, but the importance of desperation outstrips any emotional discomfort.

Powerful Men

There are a variety of open doors suitable through which the Luciferian spirit may pass. The most frequent is childhood sexual abuse. A man whose has suffered such abuse will respond in one of two ways. Depending upon the personality of the victim, he may gravitate toward effeminacy and may struggle with homosexual thoughts and behavior. Ultimately, he may succumb to the power of the devastation and gravitate toward homosexuality. Homosexuals are not born; they are created through abuse neglect or dominance.

The opposite path opens the door for the introduction of a control spirit or possibly a spirit of Lucifer. This man's life will be characterized by trying to prove that he is a man. He will act out the part of the "manly man." He will be enormously homophobic, sacrificing close male friendship so as not to appear in any way effeminate. He will be driven toward the gamut of manly pursuits. He will secretly (how ever subconsciously) fear anything that could be construed as feminine. He will probably demean girls, using them for sex alone, but never creating a loving, nurturing relationship. He must continually prove that he is tough, and strong; no weakness is allowed.

Any other type of abuse causing a boy to feel helpless and out of control may provide sufficient damage to provide a doorway for demonization. A young man who suffers under the heavy hand of an emotionless, verbally demeaning, often physically abusive father may grow up seeking control to protect himself and his fragile psyche. His own sinful nature then makes a place for such influence, as well. Fatherly neglect or a domineering mother provides as likely a doorway as the above-mentioned abuse. The coping mechanisms for trauma of any kind can easily open him up to demonization.

Curt had polio as a child. He suffered the daily application of steaming hot towels and was restricted to his bedroom while the rest of his brothers and sisters played outside. As he grew older, the effects of the polio seemed to retreat until they were barely visible. He trained himself to walk without the telltale limp and demanded of himself that the disease was non-existent.

But the polio was only the first of a one-two punch in store for Curt. He was forced to bear the shame and destruction of sexual abuse at the hands of an older, more powerful relative. The combination of these two terrible events proved too much for him. By his early teens, Curt was drinking every day. He took up smoking about the same time, because he felt it made him look tough. He soon discovered that girls could be dominated, feeding his insatiable need for control.

His life was characterized by proving he was not weak, effeminate, or homosexual. He was a man. He gravitated toward the manliest occupation he could find: heavy machinery mechanic. He went so far as to establish a side business handling high explosives. He spent most of his adult life performing fireworks shows. If anything was dangerous and manly, Curt gravitated in its direction.

Once deliverance occurred, Curt moved toward wholeness. However, as is the case with most recovering from the grip of control, he could not hear what was necessary to find true freedom. He could not hear of the fruit of the Spirit such as gentleness and meekness; it was too difficult and even foreign to his paradigm. He wanted to be in charge of ministry instead of participating as a team member. He found little satisfaction in a gentle approach to child rearing. He remained in his learned behavior until Father met him in a fresh revelation of Himself and Curt bowed to the refining fire of the Lord.

He is now one of a precious few former hosts of Luciferian spirits who have made any significant steps to wholeness.

A Rare Find

Frankly, we have not seen much success with those hosting Luciferian spirits. Oh, we are able to cast out the unclean spirit. However, success in deliverance ministry is not measured by the absence of unclean spirits, but by the level of recovery resulting in living the abundant life. Gauging success by deliverance alone is tantamount to a surgeon gauging the success of surgery by how much corrupted tissue he removed from the patient. Though this is important to the process, a better judge of the success of the operation is whether or not the patient recovers and is able to live a normal life.

One reason so few clients recover from the influence of a Luciferian spirit is the connection between the unclean spirit's purpose and the presence of inherent authority in the man. The path to wholeness is characterized by vulnerability. Men are reluctant to make themselves vulnerable for any reason. Counselors and therapists know how difficult it is to get a man to come for marriage counseling, and then, to get him to open up his feelings. Any real man will tell you: if something is wrong, he can fix it himself. He will oppose anything suggesting he may be inadequate or ignorant. Men take care of themselves. Women and children are weak and need his help. He will refuse to admit his weakness.

When a man carrying a Luciferian spirit undergoes deliverance, he exposes himself to a reality heretofore entirely unknown. It is the domain of vulnerability. He has been trained since early in his life that he must maintain control and authority in every situation so he preserves safety, security and protection. The first movement toward wholeness is like the pendulum of a clock. He will swing from total control toward the opposite extreme. This new position will exemplify the exact opposite of control: fear, uncertainty, and vulnerability. He may submit himself to it temporarily, but inevitably, there comes a moment when he will demand that he is "whole" so the vulnerability will disappear. Because of his natural level of authority, he will be less likely to subject himself to the demands of the wholeness process. He will convince himself he is fixed and it is time to move on. This is the nature of self-surrender. Strong men are less likely to be willing to surrender.

Another obstacle to achieving a substantial level of wholeness is the problem of submission to authority. No self respecting host of a Luciferian spirit would submit to the authority of a weak, passive, or sensitive person, especially in the spiritual realm. Most of the Luciferian spirits we have encountered have been in churches either pastored by men who host Luciferian spirits themselves, or surprisingly enough, pastored by men whose wives host control spirits and consequently exhibit one level of Ahab's nature or another. Remember, Ahab is a king. Just because his wife is usurping his authority does not mean he does not exhibit kingly authority toward others. Therefore, the host of a Luciferian spirit will gravitate toward this high level of authority.

Without a high level of spiritual authority being exercised, the man infected by this spirit is lost. He cannot and will not submit to some weakling pastor for whom he has no respect. When deliverance occurs for him, he must be urged to submit to the probing work of the Holy Spirit through a man he respects. If one is not available, we frequently offer ourselves in this position through email and phone counseling. However, due to the dearth of true spiritual authority within the structured church, we are reluctant to provide deliverance for fear of Matthew 12:43-45 coming to pass. *"When an evil spirit comes out of a man, it goes through arid places seeking rest and does not find it. Then it says, 'I will return to the house I left.' When it arrives, it finds the house unoccupied, swept clean and put in order. Then it goes and takes with it seven other spirits more wicked than itself, and they go in and live there. And the final condition of that man is worse than the first."*

LUCIFER ON THE LOOSE

One of the most fascinating experiences we have had with a Luciferian spirit happened in an associate's church. At the end of the meeting, David, a retired pastor, was assisting in praying for those who had responded and was praying for a young pregnant woman. One of the leadership team of the church (we will call him Andy) asked permission to pray for the young woman after David was finished. Andy was the stepfather of the young lady. He touched her very pregnant stomach and pronounced, "This is my child." His voice was inordinately gruff and deep. He fell to the floor, writhing and speaking in this demonic voice. The elderly pastor, not hearing very well, told us later that he assumed the man was speaking in tongues under the power of the Holy Spirit, so he continued praying for the next person in line, paying little attention to Andy's antics.

Suddenly, Andy made a couple of extraordinary leaps and landed against the opposite wall of the sanctuary. He was crouched in an aggressive, football-like pose facing David. He shouted, "I will kill you!" in the frighteningly demonic voice, and raced across the front of the church and leaped at David. They both tumbled to the floor in a heap. Andy kept shouting as he climbed over the stunned pastor, trying to reach his throat to strangle him. At this point, those milling around, many of whom I had trained in spiritual warfare and deliverance, finally figured out that this might be demonic and rescued the elderly pastor from his attacker.

When the limping, retired pastor explained it to him, Andy submitted to deliverance. I got a call that afternoon to take Andy through deliverance. In the pre-deliverance interview, Andy shared with the counselor that he was unaware of what he had done. This is called lost time. When a demonized person becomes extremely passive to its control, the demon may block the conscious memory of its host while executing some vile scheme. The person is thus unaware anything has happened. This was the case with Andy.

During the session, we encountered an obstacle very difficult to overcome. As we were commanding the spirit to go, it stopped and refused to move further. I worked for a few minutes and nothing happened. As I asked the Holy Spirit to explain it to me, I leaned over to the team member to my left and said, "Uh, oh." He said, "What do you mean, 'Uh, oh?" Before I could respond, Andy (though not Andy's voice) said, "It's because you're too f'ing soft." He was taunting me, trying to demean me and take control of the session.

Following his deliverance, Andy had no recollection of those events. However, he progressed nicely on his journey to wholeness. At one point, his wife phoned out of concern that she had discovered him on the couch in the fetal position weeping uncontrollably. He was experiencing fear and confusion and was unable to function. Though this condition was temporary, within the first year after his deliverance, Andy decided that he was whole enough and his journey abruptly came to an end.

One significant point made during the deliverance session

came when I was explaining how the wholeness process would likely affect Andy. He understood immediately. He asked if it would affect his job. He was a loan negotiator for a bank. He was responsible to literally go to war with lending institutions to obtain money for his bank. He knew right off the description of the first stage of the wholeness process would incapacitate his cutthroat approach to business and render him too weak to perform his duties. He agreed to continue with the session even with this knowledge. Later, it turned out to greatly affect his job performance, so he put a stop to the wholeness process in favor of his job.

In the end, he was unwilling to remain vulnerable and he sat down on his journey. One day he announced to his pastor, "I'm healed." Though his learned behavior was still ingrained, he could no longer tolerate his own weakness. The rest of the story is typical of many men who have been delivered from Luciferian spirits. Andy ran from those who were assisting him in his recovery to take back control of his life.

Chapter 16

Weapons of Control Spirits

The Spirit of Superiority

The spirit of Jezebel and the spirit of Lucifer have many aspects in common. They are the apex of control in each gender and mirror many evil characteristics. However, they have one other aspect in common. Since the functions of these demons target those around them, they falsely elevate the self-image of their hosts to the place of superiority. To conceal the intimidation the host experiences at the hands of the unclean spirit, he/she frequently overcompensates. This may be identified psychologically as a defense mechanism. However, within the parameters of the Kingdom of Light, it can be more clearly explained as a destructive spiritual response.

The host of each type of control spirit, as well as the spirits of Jezebel and Lucifer, are driven to bring his/her life into some semblance of control. As has been said repeatedly, the doorway for demonization is most often some sort of trauma. There are many such avenues of infiltration by unclean spirits, each generating corrupt control and consuming harassment into his/her existence. The result of such manipulation by control spirits creates a sense of worthlessness, unworthiness, and an impression that he/she is unloved or unlovable.

Therefore, the victim's instinct for self-preservation will demand action. *Enter the spirit of superiority.* The resident ruling demons convince the host that they must give the impression that they are superior to the people they are seeking to control. This most often appears to be an inner sense rather than a conscious operation. So, since the person is unaware of the presence of the demon, a conscious perception of his/her air of superiority will also be lacking.

THE GENDER SPHERE

There are three general spheres in which the spirit of Superiority functions. The first is in the area of gender. A female host of a control or Jezebel spirit is likely to be a man-hater, even if she appears to be very submissive. A concealed dark pool of bitterness often provides the resource for maintaining the presence of the spirit. The woman will be trained by the demon to manipulate and demean the male of the species so that her sense of inferiority is kept in check. She will be driven to control and manipulate out of a sense of helping the target of her control. She may outwardly submit, but inwardly, she will burn.

Cliff owns a business and his wife Sharon works with him. Cliff is the boss and provides leadership to keep the business going. We were out to dinner with them when Sharon related this story. One day, Cliff was correcting one of their female employees. As Cliff turned and walked away, Sharon stepped up to the dejected woman and gave her some wisdom learned over many years of working with her husband. She told the lady, "Just tell him you understand what he is saying to you and then do what I have always done. As he is walking away from you, just say, 'Jerk!' under your breath, so that he cannot hear you. That always makes me feel better."

Sharon's feelings of worthlessness and unworthiness demanded protective action. Though to the casual observer, she appeared submissive, Sharon was actually convinced that she was superior to that stupid, stupid man. She could not endure the sense of inferiority. She was driven to rise above her attacker and take back control. Her responses, under the tutelage of her control spirit, help to provide security, stability, and comfort when her emotions threatened to spin out of control.

The male version of the spirit of Superiority simply drives its host to dominate women. Any woman in legitimate authority over him is an automatic target of antagonism. Moreover, all females must be subjected through intimidation and domination. Out of his severe sense of inferiority, the male host of a control spirit dreads his own insignificance and is therefore driven to dominate women. This is much of the warped rationale for spousal abuse. The wife of a person manifesting a control spirit will be subjected to what might appear to be multiple personalities resident in her husband. He may be caring and loving one minute and fly into an uncontrollable rage the next. As with all victims of trauma, his emotions will be out of control and when he feels insecurity, he will respond, not with a cry for help, but with a leap "above" the woman who intimidates him. He may beat her physically, verbally, or emotionally in order to regain safety for his corrupted self-image. In this manner, the resident unclean spirit provides a semblance of comfort, safety and protection in return for rulership of the person.

In both cases, men and women develop an inner sense that they are really above those who relentlessly make them feel inferior. In the end, comfort is provided by an unclean spirit to maintain that superiority by enabling the manipulative edge in the victim's life.

THE RELIGIOUS SPHERE

Another flaw of those hosting the spirit of Superiority is in the arena of religion. Christianity, allegedly the exercise of the love of Father upon the earth, is crippled by division. It is fascinating that each time a new move of God explodes upon the earth, when the proponents of the former move become angry and expend tremendous energy defending their doctrines against the onslaught of the "new" thing.

The Fundamentalists distain the Evangelicals; the Evangelicals distain the Pentecostals; the Pentecostals distain the Charismatics; and the Charismatics distain the Renewalists. The Renewalists are so busy repelling the attacks of the rest of the Church, they are being distracted from what Father is trying to do through them. As has been the case throughout Church history, Father must turn His attention from these groups--each convinced of the superiority of their own pet revelation—and manifest Himself to another group outside the institutionalized Church to keep the Message moving.

Our arrogance is astonishing.

Each time Father visits the earth, the spirit of Superiority enters into the mix to destroy, not through the obvious means of blatant sin, but through what appears to be the most spiritual of deeds: defending the Faith. However, Father is forever moving, unveiling more of Himself to His people. The fact that we are like little mice huddled in the corner of our denominational distinctives does not deter Him from His objective. He simply moves away from what He did, continuing to *do*. The Faith is ever expanding as He reveals more of Who He is.

Pastor Joel is a Nazarene. His family history is replete with Nazarene clergy. He is proud of his heritage. When we met, Joel was suspicious of anything his denomination deemed "Pentecostal." Though I was not a Pentecostal, I still unsettled Joel. I was fascinated by the "persecution" that Joel perceived coming from Pentecostals. Each time he felt attacked in his doctrinal position, he was forced to prove the superiority of his doctrine. He could not take being made to feel inferior to them.

Even more fascinating was Joel's opinion of Baptists. Though he felt abused by the Pentecostals, he gladly professed his own superiority to anything "Baptist." It was as if he had an instinct for where he stood in the religious pecking order and, while hating the pecking he took from those "above" him, he was very pleased with himself to peck at those he viewed to be "below."

As we developed relationship outside the cell walls of the traditional Church, Joel and I began taking chances with our newfound friendship and began arguing doctrine. Over time, we discovered that, though we were at doctrinal extremes, we formed a trust bond that superseded any of our differences. Today he is my best friend and there is no place for the spirit of Superiority in our relationship.

The presence of a Jezebelian or Luciferian spirit guarantees the illusion of doctrinal and theological superiority. The people will know that they are more spiritual than the leadership of their church. They will press for positions of greater responsibility within the structure to ensure the purity of the group. Their motives will appear selfless and Godly while the reality is simple satisfaction of their need to remain superior.

THE RACE SPHERE

The final arena of influence directed by the spirit of Superiority is race. From the moment the curse was pronounced upon mankind at the Tower of Babel (Genesis 11), racism has surged through our veins. Suspicion, aggression, and arrogance fill our hearts as we look disparagingly upon those who are not like us.

Recently, I heard an African-American standup comic relate his observations of how people greet each other. He imitated two white guys approaching one another on the street. Each nodded in the direction of the other, dropping their heads in a downward manner. Of course, he dramatized it humorously, speaking in what typified a very dorky, "white guy" sort of manner.

Then, he told how different it would be for two African-American men in the same situation. He imitated their typical greeting by tilting his chin up in the air. He added some exaggerated gang-like moves to make it funny, but the point was painfully obvious. The simple act of greeting one another has become an expression of the demand for recognition in the face of oppressing cultural norms.

Every race has a natural bent toward superiority; it is built into our corrupted collective psyche. Yet, when inhabited by unclean spirits, the result is frequently deadly. Race riots, demonstrations for the simple right of equality characterized the 1960's and 1970's. Through the sacrifice of such giants as Martin Luther King and others, much was accomplished. Yet the heart of man remains stolid to the plight of those he surmises to be inferior.

Within the Church, the spirit of Superiority has preserved the natural human tendency magnificently. Instead of reaching across racial barriers and loving one another as Jesus might in our culture, Sunday morning remains the most segregated time of the week. Thankfully, some have made the leap and created an accepting atmosphere where diversity does not demand division. However, most churches cannot overcome such an onslaught.

In the host of a spirit of Jezebel or the spirit of Lucifer, the natural human tendency may produce the harvest of spiritual abuse. Since the demand for absolute authority is at the core of the nature of these two spirits, exercising abuse against other races is instinctive. This explains how the terrorists of the KKK are able cultivate the culture of hatred against Blacks and Jews under the guise of religious pietism. The spirit of Superiority was clearly at work through these men.

If the Church is to reach the rest of the world, the spirit of Racism, and the spirit of Superiority must be overthrown within our hearts first and then in the nature of our gatherings. Impotent programs like the recent Reconciliation movement only entrenched our sense of racial superiority by pacifying the guilt of the past with empty religious exercises. In effect, as the man said, "Been there; did that" and we moved back into our segregated religious communities satisfied that we've done all that was required.

All is definitely *not* well.

THE ANSWER

The only answer to all these issues is deliverance from the dominion of darkness that still pervades the unbelieving parts of our hearts. Most of us mean well, but the results are found to be sadly wanting. If *"He must increase, but I must decrease"* (John 3:30 KJV) the spirit of Superiority must have no place in your life. Once deliverance is accomplished, then the thrill ride of wholeness is before you. Pursue Father and pursue humility. *"Do not think of yourself more highly than you ought, but rather think of yourself with sober judgment, in accordance with the measure of faith God has given you"* (Romans 12:3). This word is not for others, but for you.

SCRUTINIZE YOURSELF AND PRAY FOR OTHERS

Perhaps the control issues related in this book do not resonate with you. To discover the vast array of demonic influence in other areas of your life, please order a copy of *Prophetic Deliverance* through www.bcrcamp.com.

Freedom is the issue and Jesus is the focus.

If what you have read in these pages causes you to think about some other person, take some time and look inward at your own issues. Do not use this material to exercise control over someone else. Point your finger at yourself; point your prayers toward others with this goal in the forefront of your mind:

> *"The Spirit of the Lord is upon me, because he hath anointed me to preach the gospel to the poor; he hath sent me to heal the brokenhearted, to preach deliverance to the captives, and recovering of sight to the blind, to set at liberty them that are bruised, to preach the acceptable year of the Lord"* (Luke 4:18-19 KJV).

About the Author

Tim Mather, Th.D., is the founder and executive director of Bear Creek Ranch, a retreat center focusing on deliverance and wholeness ministry. He is the author of *Prophetic Deliverance: The Missing Ministry of Jesus in the Church* and *Escaping Church: A Guide to Life Outside the Institution*. He can be contacted at www.BCRcamp.com.

BEAR CREEK RANCH
Deliverance & Wholeness Retreats

Pursuing inner healing before deliverance is like putting the cart before the horse.

Jesus' mission statement in Luke 4: 18-19 KJV includes the six supernatural elements of life in Christ: discovery of the good news of Kingdom life, healing for the brokenness, freedom from demonic influences, new spiritual sight, liberty from Kingdom of Darkness thinking and the revelation that we are now Father's favorite. None of them are automatic upon entrance to the Kingdom of Light. Rather, the revelations must be pursued, the healing apprehended, the sight revealed. Therefore, each and every person making their way into the Kingdom needs deliverance.

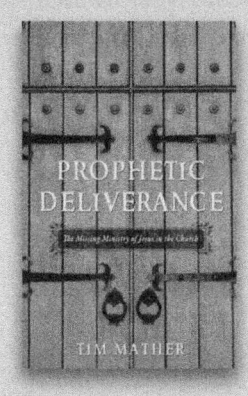

Read *Prophetic Deliverance* by Tim Mather for an up-close view of this tool for freedom from demonization.

Tim and Katie Mather seek to provide a place for people to come and receive the ministry of Deliverance and Inner Healing, through seminars and workshops at Bear Creek Ranch.

Visit www.BCRcamp.com for retreat information.

Deliverance Retreat

Wholeness Retreat

Resources

Books:

Prophetic Deliverance
by Tim Mather

Escaping Church
by Tim Mather

The Five Wholeness Steps
by Katie Mather

Supernatural Superheroes
by Heather Trim

Audio Teachings:

Upside Down Kingdom Weapons
with Tim Mather

Wholeness JumpStart
with Katie Mather

Visit the Bear Creek Bookstore for more information.
www.BCRcamp.com

Notes

[1] William J. Gaither, *He Touched Me*, (Gaither Music, 1963).

[2] M. Scott Peck, *People of the Lie*, (New York: Simon and Schuster, 1983), 39-40

[3] David A. Seamands, *Freedom From the Performance Trap*, (New York: Inspirational Press, 1988), 394.

[4] Tim Mather, *Prophetic Deliverance*, (Rockmart, GA, TrimVentures Publishing, 2018), 57.

[5] C. Fred Dickson, Demon Possession and the Christian, (Chicago: The Moody Bible Institute, 1987), 34.

[6] Robert A. Lund, The Way Church Ought To Be, (Albany, Oregon: Outside the Box Press, 2001), 53.

[7] Robert S. Magee, The Search For Significance, (Nashville, Tennessee: Word Publishing, 1998), 64.

[8] New York State Sheriff's Association Pamphlet, The Silent Scream of Child Abuse, Personal Safety and Security Series (Troy, NY)

[9] Dan Allender, The Wounded Heart, seminar, Horseheads, NY, 3-5 April 1997.

[10] Teresa Diaz-Maldonado, Recovery interview by author, Chicago, Illinois. May 2002.

[11] H. Norman Wright, Making Peace With Your Past, (Old Tappan, NJ: Fleming H. Revell Company, 1985), 23.

[12] David Johnson and Jeff VanVondersen, The Subtle Power of Spiritual Abuse, (Minneapolis, Minnesota: Bethany House Publishers, 1991), 184.

¹³Mic Hunter, Abused Boys, (New York: Ballantine Books, 1990), 59.

¹⁴Dr. Kevin Leman, The Pleasers, (Old Tappan, NJ: Fleming H. Revell Company, 1987), 7-9.

¹⁵Melody Beattie, Codependent No More, (San Francisco: Harper Collins Publishers, 1987), 36.

¹⁶Dr. Henry Cloud and Dr. John Townsend, Boundaries, (Grand Rapids, Michigan: Zondervan Publishing House, 1992), 51.

¹⁷Sandra L. Brown, Counseling Victims of Violence, (Alexandria, VA: the American Association For Counseling and Development, 1991), 165.

¹⁸Marc Dupont, Walking Out of Spiritual Abuse, (Tonbridge, Kent, England: Sovereign World Ltd., 1997), 103.

¹⁹C. Peter Wagner, Confronting the Queen of Heaven, (Colorado Springs, CO: Wagner Institute for Practical Ministry, 1998), 16-17.

²⁰Herbert Lockyer, D.D., R.S.L., F.R.G.S., All the Kings and Queens of the Bible, (Grand Rapids, Michigan: Zondervan Publishing House, 1961), 236.

²¹Rev. H.D.M. Spence, M.A., D.D., The Pulpit Commentary, Volume 5, I & II Kings, (Grand Rapids, Michigan: Wm. B. Eerdmans Publishing Company, 1950), 374.

²²Spence, The Pulpit Commentary, 377.

²³Spence, The Pulpit Commentary, 377.

²⁴C.E. Kiel, F. Delitzsch, Commentary on the Old Testament, Volume 3, (Grand Rapids, Michigan: William B. Eerdmans Publishing Company, 1975), 228.

²⁵Bree M. Keyton, ThD., D.C.E., Jezebel vs. Elijah, (Chula Vista, CA: Black Forest Press, 2001), 74.

²⁶Keyton, Jezebel vs. Elijah, 150.

Made in the USA
Columbia, SC
20 May 2018